AFTER ALAMEIN
Prisoner of War Diaries 1942-45

Paul Kingsford

The Book Guild Ltd.
Sussex, England

The Book Guild Ltd.
25 High Street,
Lewes, Sussex

First published 1992
© Paul Kingsford 1992
Set in Baskerville
Typesetting by Southern Reproductions (Sussex)
East Grinstead, Sussex
Printed in Great Britain by
Antony Rowe Ltd.
Chippenham, Wiltshire.

A catalogue record for this book is
available from the British Library

ISBN 0 86332 735 4

CONTENTS

LIST OF ILLUSTRATIONS

PREFACE

Some parts of the diary are written in code in case the Germans got hold of them. 'Goons' were Germans, 'canary' was a secret radio, 'ARA' was Air Raid alarm, 'bashing' was eating food which should have been eaten in a few days time! L.C. letter card; snooper ferret or German who looked all round inside camp; 'bully marks' camp money; KLIM powdered Canadian milk; Itie or Ite Italian.

*To many Kiwi,
Aussie and South African
friends.*

HOW I WAS CAPTURED

I was Platoon Commander in 1st/5th QRR (Queens Royal Regiment), 131 Brigade, XIII Corps, at Alamein. We crossed 'February' minefield but were pinned down by machine gun fire and tanks on the night of 24/10/42. We had had casualties crossing the minefields from A/P mines and counter-battery work.

The 1st/6th QRR were on our left but were being heavily mortared during the 25th. No tanks got through to support us as the gap in the minefield was being enfiladed from El Himeimat ('two pimples') which had been recaptured by the Germans.

The first sign of hope was when in the evening Italian parachutists in front of my platoon surrendered. I was short of men and sent my runner (Keohane by name) back with twenty-odd POWs!

The 1st/6th battalion thought we were being made prisoners and, as a result of heavy mortar fire, they were captured. After this, all the mortars came on us and we had severe casualties. We could not go forward as German parachutists had taken over the Italian pill boxes, so Colonel East decided to make a dash back when darkness came, but things got so bad that he and a handful left before dark.

I had been shot through the leg and shrapnel went into my left thigh, and I was picked up next morning and taken to enemy trenches in the rear (which we had passed earlier). When I got up, I noticed a mortar bomb stuck in the rock an inch or two from my head! It had not gone off and, in retrospect, I realized I had been temporarily unconscious when it had landed!

After a hair-raising journey in an ambulance dodging shells, I was deposited for three days in a triangle of wire. Then

I was taken back with some Aussies and Canadians to Sidi Barrani, Tobruk and Derna from where we were flown to Italy. The Canadian Airmen had some mad scheme to take over the Caproni Aircraft, but fortunately they eventually realized that we would have had no hope as the sentries were armed! I was taken to Bari Hospital.

TIME IN HOSPITAL

At Bari I was in a ward with about two dozen British prisoners. I had a high temperature and was not eating till after the operation on my thigh, and cannot remember much about anything.

We were taken by ambulance later to Altamura Hospital where we survived on two very small bowls of rice and water or spaghetti and water plus a bread roll. On Christmas Day we got a tangerine. I was glad to get to Bari Camp (after ten weeks in hospital) as we got an occasional Red Cross parcel there.

1942

---

21 October. Got to know (of our attack). Demonstration at night. Wrote home.

22 October. Communion. Packed up. V. busy. Moved up after meal in evening. Dug positions in front of Arty.

23 October. Attack began in evening. Barrage.

24 October. Moved up for night attack. Over 'February'. Bullet through right leg.

25 October. Mortars. Hell! 2 bits of shrapnel. Left ear deaf. Many miraculous escapes. East etc. went before dusk.

26 October. Picked up by Italians. Shelled by own Arty in front line. By Ambulance to triangle of wire. Cross-examined in middle of night.

27 October. Set off by lorry. Back again to triangle. (I only had 1 blanket.)

28 October. Set off by lorry. Back again to triangle.

29 October. Daba cage – eventually!!

30 October. Mersa Matruh. Long wait on way there. Capt. Jones (AA) & SA (Prior, Reg) there. Given sack (with fleas!!) by Arab (sack welcome as blanket but bitten all over!). Bottle of tonic water between three of us from SA natives.

31 October. Bardia. Bumpy journey there!! Patrick (E.R. of New Brunswick, Canada), John Mills (Whitby) and others joined us here.

1 November. Bumpy journey to Tobruk.

2 November. Tobruk. Aussies joined us.

3 November. Derna.

4 November. Shower and disinfestation. V. welcome. Air to Lecce.

5 November. 1st class train to Bari. Walked to camp 75.

7 November. Rt thigh v. painful. Night in camp hospital.

8 November. Ospedale militare, Bari.

9-20 November. Temperature up (Highest 41). Off food.

11 November. Reported missing.

2 December. Operation (V. painful for 5 days)

4 December. Reported POW.

11 December. Altamura. Ambulance.

13 December. Bleeding stopped. Only pus now.

14 December. Doctor strapped my wound up (in together). Officers in hospital:– Graham Bryton, Olly Olpherts, Bill Wadmore, Pat Wilson, Gordon Rolandson, Harold Drinkwater, Peter Tivey, Oswald C.B. Cole-Biroth, Gordon Smith.

20 December. My card (d. Nov 8) home.

22 December. Letter (d. Nov 18) home.

31 December. Pat (R.C.A.F.), Archie Ainsley, Pete Moloney arrived.

1943

6 **January.** My first walk round room. V. groggy!!

8 January. C.B., Bill, Gordon and Pat W. left for camp. Other interesting things at hospital:–

Cappellano (D, Francesco Julis)!!
Hot water twice a day for tea, cocoa etc.
Parcels for 3 weeks (1 in 15) until they ran out.

28 January. Campo P.G.75 in Bari by train from Altamura Hospital with Olly, Graham, Smith.

29 January. Sent P.C. home.

1 February. Went to matins with Olly. I stayed for communion.

2 February. Letter-card (d.23 Dec) from Aunt Vera. Wrote home. *Discourses of Epictetus* (Arrian) translated by George Long. Good book.

3 February. Beat Olly and Bill 3 times each at chess.

4 February. Beat Bill (2-1) and Olly (1) at chess. Letters (dated 21 & 23 from M & D), V.G. Concert at night.

5 February. Beat Olly 2-0 at chess.

6 February. Sent P.C. home. Beat Bill at chess. *Reflections on the French Revolution* by Edmund Burke. Rather dry book!!

7 February. Church. Lovely day. Beat Olly & Bill at chess. Drew a game to each.

8 February. Funeral (2 Yugoslavs). Beat Olly & Bill several times at chess.

9 February. Funeral (y.s) Letter (d. Dec 15 Red X, Rome) from M. Beat Olly 2-0. *Triumphant Pilgrimage* – Owen Rutter. V. good book about an Englishman's pilgrimage to Mecca.

10 February. Wrote letter-card home. Fine day. Red X parcel issue started on ratio of one per week (ie bulk) 1 kilo of

14

jam issued from Mess.

11 February. Inoculation for diphtheria. Rainy day. Letter dated 30th Dec from Mummy. *Lord Tony's Wife* – Baroness Orczy. Good book.

12 February. Sent P.C. home. Drew with Bill (Wadmore) 1-1 at chess.

13 February. Lovely weather. My parcel day. (Contents 2 tins of sausages. 1 Galantine, 1 Salmon, 1 bar chocolate, 1 tin margarine, 1 tin jam, 1 tin cheese, 1 biscuits (Peak Frean's).) Beat Bill at chess & drew a game. Beat Olly twice. *The Murders in Praed Street* by John Rhode. V. good book. Was sick at night (Salmon?).

21 February. Holy Communion. Evensong at 2.00 (was late). Windy but sunny day. Sports finals in the afternoon. The Band was in attendance. Watched some very amusing pillow-fights. Two clowns there as well. The Yugoslav Officer arrived from a German prison camp. lira sweets in the canteen. Lecture in evening by Padre Letcher (S.A.) on 'Some old Christian Documents Discovered in the Middle East' – in reality the history of the documents that went to make up the Bible. *Victoria the Great* – Edith Sitwell. Excellent book & very interesting.

22 February. Potatoes for breakfast!! Gave lecture on 'Iceland' in evening. Small search. French lessons in morning & Fr. conversation in afternoon. Air raid warning just after we went to bed. 'All Clear' went – followed by another warning. Then I went to sleep & so did not hear the guns.

23 February. French lesson in morning. Fine day. Wine in the canteen. Got a litre of vino. So did George Crookenden (Nephew of the Col. at 167 OCTU!!) & we had his litre heated up with sugar and orange in the evening. We had mine the night after tomorrow. A glass of Vermouth in the mess in evening. V. good.

24 February. Lovely day. French lesson in afternoon. Beat Bill at chess. Musical concert in the evening. V. good. Glass of Vermouth in the mess. Wrote letter-card home.

25 February. French lesson in afternoon. *Return via Dunkirk* by Gun Buster. Quite good, but nothing special.

26 February. Played Smithy deck-tennis for half an hour at 9.30. V. warm work! The Papal Nuncio paid us a visit (for Xmas). Paraded for him & waited about a long time before he arrived. Sunny but windy. French lesson in afternoon. Beat Olly 2-0 at chess.

27 February. Letter 6 (d. 10 Jan 1943) from Mummy. My first complete parcel – a Canadian one containing:– Salmon, Bully Meat Roll, Sardines, Butter (1 lb), Orange Marmalade, Biscuits, Cheese, raisins, prunes, sugar, tea, Klim powdered milk, chocolate (milk), salt and soap. Made excellent pudding – chocolate, raisins, an apple, Klim, sugar, butter, bread-crumbs and biscuit!! Also made fish-cakes (of salmon) which I fried in the evening with some onions!! The Italian Commandant assembled all officers in Recreation Room in afternoon to explain why some of the complaints we made to the Papal Nuncio could not be rectified!! Drew Olly 1-1 at chess!! Glass of vino in Mess. *Beau Brocade* by Baroness Orczy – V. good book.

28 February. Sunny day with a little wind. Holy Communion, & Evensong at 2.00. The little S.A.O.R. took them as usual. He had joined up as an Ambulance Driver in the Union. Sent P.C. home. Made similar pudding to yesterday's but no chocolate. However, I put a prune and a little wine in it!! Not so good as yesterday's.

1 March. Fine but windy. Shower-baths not v. hot. The Ites (Italians) wanted to see me at 3pm. They had a letter to Ospedale Militare, Bari, from the Invalid's Comfort Section of the Red Cross saying that my parents were 'very worried' about my wound. They had to send back a report saying that I was now all right. French lessons in the afternoon. Made a very excellent fruit salad & cream!! Recipe:– 5 prunes, 1 apple, raisins & a little vino. Thick cream made of Klim, butter and sugar. Had it in the evening (cold), and it really was excellent. Still the usual rumours of O.R.'s and of Officer's departure to permanent camps!! *King George VI* – Taylor Derbyshire. V. interesting.

2 March. We were divided into camps. Myself, Olly, Graham, John Mills, Manders (32 in all) to camp 47. Fine day. P.C. (d. Dec 10) from Mummy. Sent letter-card home.

Oranges on sale in canteen – also onions. Hugh (Matier) gave a good lecture on the 'Development of Agriculture in England' in the evening. All the ORs except permanent staff left at night.

3 March. Gorgeous day. V. hot. French lesson in morning. Camp 35 people left at 12.00 after early lunch. Helped George Crookenden (nephew of the Col. at 167 OCTU!!) down with his kit. Made monster fruit salad to finish most of fruit off so as not to have to carry it:– 2 apples, 2 oranges, 5 prunes and raisins. Made cream for it. Had half a meat roll at lunch so I felt *very* satisfied!! Handed bedding in. Had a shave in barber's shop. Handed camp chits in (to go on credit, we hope!). Saw S.B.M.O (Capt. Thomson) about report home on my health. 'Skilly up' at 3.30. Search at 4.00. Put kit on lorry. Marched down to Bari Station at dusk. Waited about on the square outside. Got kit off lorry with surprisingly little (considering) bother. Train left between 8.30 and 9.00 and went slowly to Foggia where it remained until 5 am. Had tin of Itie Bully and a loaf issued. Slept for two short spells – altogether about 2 hours. A drunken officer promised us wine and we kept a bottle for him during the night – but we never got a drop!! Swapped eight cigarettes with a young Itie soldier for a 'loaf' of bread, as there were a crowd of them outside at Foggia. Carried on a bit of propaganda until the Itie officer (for our camp) stopped me from looking out of the carriage window!! Sleep almost impossible on account of the noise of the sentries both in and outside the compartment. 6 of us in the compartment and 2 sentries – who were quite reasonable.

4 March. Despite my second spell of sleep, I woke up very sleepy. When the lavatory was free, I got a wash etc., and then had breakfast (3/4 loaf and marmalade and butter followed by an orange). Travelled through moderately interesting country up the Adriatic coast with the sea in view for most of the time. A bit hilly in parts, and a bit more civilized than further south. Frequent requests to the sentries for wine were fruitless until we got to Ancona (I think!) when we got a bottle of vino (pseudo-Chianti) for 50 lire. We had no money originally as we had handed it in, and the Itie officer would not give our compartment any of our credits although he had given some other officers some of theirs. Consequently, one of us bartered a British blanket for 50 lire with the officer, who only handed over 45 so we took the blanket back!! However, he soon repented and 50 lire came our way!! The officer was also continually asking for our underclothes and even our trousers, but we would have none of it!! An Italian came on the train selling figs, but, as we had no money, one of our officers tried to barter a waistcoat made out of blanket!! After getting it out of his pack three times with great inconvenience, we could not get a reasonable market!! The fig man offered one packet of figs, rising to two packets, and at another visit to three, but four was the lowest we would go!! However, one of our sentries very kindly bought us a packet. Also of interest, a little boy came up and asked us for *pane* (bread), but we said that Mussolini would give him some!! The carriage was quite warm and very stuffy at one time during the first night. Our route was Foggia, Termoli Junction, Pescara Central (where some camps got out – for Chieti – including Pat), Civitanova Marche, Ancona (where we got an electric train tacked on), Bologna (where we changed compartments twice – I don't know why!!) and Modena,* where we arrived at 23.15 hours. After waiting in the Waiting Room for some time, some small buses took us to Camp 47. The buses were packed but it was only a very short way. The camp was brilliantly lit.

5 March. A.M. After being checked, we were thoroughly searched for a few hours. We then drew our bedding (palliasse and 3 blankets) and bedded down on the floor of a big bay. Was very tired when I woke up after 4-1/4 hours' badly-needed sleep. Coffee, apples, orange and 'loaf' of bread brought to us before Roll Call at 9.00. Two officers had escaped, so we were kept on parade until 10.00. Put into Room 4B7 where there was a 'vacancy' with 2 Lt Colonels and 3 Majors!! (Lt Col J. M. Webb, Lt Col E. S. Thompson, Major P. S. Loeser, Major H. N. Morton and Major R. H. Hughesdon.) Moved bedding and kit across. Got bed later on. Gordon, John Mills and Manders and I had tried to get together, but it was not possible. Lunch – cauliflower, carrots, cheese and coffee. The coffee was the Italian issue but had

---

* MODENA CAMP (LG-47) This was a well laid-out camp of bungalows. Almost all the prisoners were S. Africans, New Zealanders and some Australians. We had regular Red X parcels, and the menus look even lavish. We could even get wine occasionally. I was one of the few Britons there.

milk in it, and was not unbearable like at Bari. It might be tasteless but is not distasteful!! In the morning I had drawn 100 lire from the bank. At 2.00 we went to the orderly room to give our particulars, at 4.00 to the M.O. who asked if we were all right, and at 4.30 to the library where I got *The Coloured Counties* by Charles Bradley Ford out. It had some marvellous coloured photographs of English countryside in it, and there was a good though necessary short description of each county in it. Dinner – bully, cauliflower and carrots. Also fruit. Had ration of Marsala at 4.30 pm.

6 March. Early roll call at 8.00. Breakfast – fruit, bread and coffee. Read most of morning. Lunch – salmon, cauliflower, onion and lentil soup – also fruit. Drew a parcel (chocolate, sugar, margarine, orange marmalade, condensed milk, 'so-tastee' cheese, and tin of biscuits). System at this camp of taking meats, tea, etc. out of parcels, and going into the mess – a good system provided a check is kept and we get all food cooked at meal times, also it goes further. We have tea brought to bungalows at 10.30 am and 3.30 pm and hot water at 8.30 pm. Went to the library in afternoon. Lt Col Webb drew *Coloured Counties* out for painting view etc. Went to 'pub' at 4.30 and had ration of Vermouth (6L). Also shared a bottle of sparkling wine with Manders and John. Crowded room, and real pubby atmosphere!! Dinner – meat, cauliflower, onions and fig rice. Sent a P.C. home.

11 March. Breakfast – bread, coffee, fruit, jam. V. cold day. Wrote letter home. Filled more of diary in. Formed French Group with Capts Stanton and Thompson amongst others – 5 in all. We shall be working together, as all are of same standard. Took *Forsyte Saga* Vol II by John Galsworthy back to the library. Very good book. Enjoyed it. Walked about with Major Hughesdon before lunch – vegetable soup (v.g.), curried onions, and fruit. Capt Thompson persuaded me to write an article in the 'Out Crop', so I started one on 'Iceland' in the afternoon! Got a forage cap and B.D. trousers (too small) from the clothing store. Had the ration of marsala at the canteen. The band was playing. Crowded as usual.

13 March. Warm and sunny again. Shaved, Went on walk at 10.00 – about 3 miles and far enough! V. warm. Read my book when back. Lunch – onions and cheese. Started 'fair copy' of Iceland which I finished after dinner. Had a hot shower after 5. Roll call. Dinner – pasta asciuta and cauliflower. Had talk with two S. Africans after dinner (Capt Turner & ?) over a marsala. Had 'soup' (similar to marmite) in the evening. I had bought 10 at lira each from the canteen.

14 March. Twins' birthday. V. warm and sunny. Went to Communion at 8.15. Collected my breakfast (stewed apples and honey) afterwards. Roll call at 9 instead of 8. Went to Matins at 10 with John. Good sermon about part of our duty to God and what he did for us. 'Gladiators' meeting afterwards. Nothing much except number of teams in each sport decided. Checked over my 'proof' (of article) before lunch (meat roll, carrots, white turnips and soup). Read and sunbathed (!!) in afternoon. Also completed diary to date. No roll call. Dinner – pot roast and tomatoes, fried onions, cauliflower, stewed apples and rice, toasted cheese (leather!) and coffee. Excellent meal. Went to 'United Services' service at 7.40. Read in evening. V. good cup of cocoa.

15 March. New arrival (a naval chap) at breakfast – picked up on 23rd Feb. Parcels arrived! 25 players issued (issue). Finished my book – *The Silver Spoon* by John Galsworthy. It takes up his story from Vol III of *Forsyte Saga* (which I got out of the library today). V. good book. Lunch – sardines and onions. Lovely day again. Got walnuts (15) from the canteen (£6). Read in the sun in the afternoon. Meeting for those interested in gardening after 5.00 roll call. Peter Manders, John Mills and I formed a syndicate. Nothing much decided. Had ration of marsala. Dinner – boiled beef with a suspicion of dumplings and carrots, cauliflower and cream rice. Turned cold at night. Had talk with Col Webb.

☆ ☆ ☆

17 March. Went on walk at 9.45. Went the usual way down the main road for about an hour. Lovely day again. Read in the morning. Lunch – meat roll and baked beans. Took B.D.

trousers to the tailors in afternoon. Got a bottle of orangeade and some walnuts. Received 6 letters!! – 2 from Daddy (dated Jan 7 and 28), and letters from Mummy (Jan 3), Uncle Charlie (Jan 21), Aline (Jan 12) and Margaret (Jan 5). Daddy said that he had told New Bodleian Library to send me Classical books and course of study. I do not yet know whether Classics or History is better. Finished reading *Forsyte Saga* (Vol III) – Awakening and to let. V. good book. Got *The Reformation in England* by F. M. Pariche out of the library. Got some vino from the canteen, after I had had a hot shower. (No pressure of water at first.) Dinner – pasta asciuta and cauliflower. Read letters and made lists out etc. in evening.

20 March. Went on the walk – down the main road as usual. Lunch – meat roll and cauliflower. Went to a lecture by Capt Penly on the Alamein Show. Good lecture. Started making notes on *The Reformation in England*. Slow work! Dinner – pasta asciuta and cauliflower. Went for a shower after roll call, but the water pressure was not on, so I had one at 7.45 pm. Made some more notes on the Reformation.

21 March. Went to Communion at 7.15. Porridge for breakfast. Went to Matins on the verandah at 10.00. Made some more notes out before lunch (cheese, cauliflower and carrots). Went to the Sunday afternoon entertainment in the square in 6 block. The band opened with a selection of classical jazz. Then 'News Pointers of the Week' by 'Dimbleby'. Pianoforte duet. 'Professional Tennis' by Alan Steadman – a champion N.Z. and Wimbledon player. Light music by orchestra. 'Tribal Customs of S.A. Natives'. And the band played selection of dance music, while we had tea and a piece of cake each. The news and tennis lecture were excellent. So was 'Tribal Customs', but it was far too long. Frequent interruptions by electric train behind. Made some more notes on Reformation before and after dinner. Steak and dumpling, cauliflower, boiled onions and rice pudding. Good meal.

25 March. Read a lot of poems out of *Oxford Book of English Verse*

– mainly of Shelley and Keats. (I had read Milton's last night). Did a bit of brisk walking round the camp after tea at 10.30 and then continued with my notes. Finished my notes off in the afternoon. Took book back to the library and got *King's Treasuries of Literature* by Sir A. T. Quiller-Couch *(Standard English Prose from Fisher to Galsworthy)*. Very interested in *Reformation in England,* and knew it pretty well after taking notes. V. well written book. An officer diagnosed as having meningitis – indoor gatherings prohibited. Read in the evening.

Several days' entries consisting of names and dates of authors read have been excised. They show the range of books available and the author's growing interest in English literature and its many byways.

29 March. Got up one hour earlier, as we had put the clocks forward last night. Roll call inside (both times) as it was very wet. Also cold and dreary day. Read *Sir Walter Raleigh* most of the day. Repatriation candidates getting ready to go. All naval personnel on order to move – rumours of their being repatriated (!). Peter Manders amongst them (as he was Fleet Air Arm). This combined with the weather made one feel very 'browned-off' and miserable!! 20 cigarettes issued in the morning. Had marsala with John, Peter, Graham and a N. Zealander. Walnuts from canteen.

30 March. Wet rainy day again. Went to lecture on 'Literature'. V. good as usual – dealing mostly with the Restoration dramatists (Etherege, Wycherley and Congrave), and the beginning of the novel incl. Bunyan. Went to lecture on 'History of Architecture' dealing rather sketchily with Anglo-Saxon, Norman, Early English and Decorated Gothic Architecture. Drew 200 lira out of the bank in the afternoon. Did my French sentences for Saturday. Also revised to page 57 in the Otto-Onions French Grammar. Got some toothpaste from the canteen. Said goodbye to Peter and the S.A. naval officer who sat at our table in the mess (who had just arrived). They were going to a naval camp (P.G. 35) with the two Bari 'canteen officers' and others – for repatriation? The weather cheered up a bit in the afternoon, and we had a roll call outside. The sun came out in the evening. Read a bit. Also had a shower-bath after queuing up for a long time. Wrote P.C. home.

31 March. Drew a parcel at 9.15. Consequently missed the walk, so I walked round the camp with John. Shaved. Sunny and warm day. Read a lot during the day. Lt Col Webb left with the others for repatriation. I have to go to another room if 'senior officers' want to come into the room. As they did, I saw 5 Bungalow Adjutant of New Zealanders to see if I could move in with Olly etc. Wrote letter-card home.

1 April. Moved across to 5A1 with John – to Olly's room with 17 in it. Took all morning to get fixed up. In spite of the Majors in room 6B7 trying to get me allowed to stay, I had to move. Practically impossible to read even at times with people going through continuously to the rooms beyond, and quite often a row in the room itself. However, I suppose I have been lucky to have been in a small room. Nothing special in the afternoon. Had marsala and rice with John and another. Band played. Talked to Olly about the duration of the war in Italy in the evening for a bit!! Read afterwards. RAF 25th birthday party!! (Red patches, to show we were POWs, sewn on by It. tailor in afternoon!!)

2 April. Drizzly rain first thing in morning, but sunny and warm after 10.30 although a fairly strong wind. Went on the walk. V. warm. 'Wood' fatigue while we were on the walk. Swapped tin of margarine and cheese for cocoa and 40 cigarettes at the Exchange Mart in the afternoon. Went to lecture on Greek campaign. Roll call 2.30. Read quite a lot. Some new arrivals came from camp 35. 20 in our room now.

3 April. Finished reading *Sir Walter Raleigh* by Edward Thompson. Excellent book. Enjoyed it immensely. Went to a French lesson at 9.00. Watched Gladiators beat Giants at baseball (4-5) in the afternoon. Took book back to the library and got *Catherine of Aragon* by Garrett Mattingley out. Had a shower in the evening after waiting some time – not v. good shower.

4 April. Went to Communion at 7.15. Roll call parade 'organized by the Italians' 8.00-10.45. S.B.O. Lt Col Page (committed suicide on return to N.Z. after his order to 'stay put' in Sept 1943), alarm etc! 'Words and Music' in the afternoon. Poor talk on habits of Afrikaner farmers – too long. Good talk on 'New Zealand through the Looking-glass.' Band did not play enough. Read a bit afterwards. No aft. roll call! Went to the Service with Olly at 7.40.

5 April. Long roll call – another one after an hour's break for breakfast. One man short! – found. Did my French homework in the afternoon. Went on the P.T. (for beginners) at 2.45. Short but strenuous. Felt better for it. Read in the evening. (Washed 3 prs of socks, a towel and two hankies in the morning. Walked around with (S.A.) before dinner.) Cigarette issue. Lovely day.

6 April. Literature lecture on the Augustine (Age of Reason) period with particular regard to Pope (1688-1744) the (urban) neo-classicist and his works. French at 11.00 when our two bits of translation were handed back. Dealt mainly with the pronouns. Read in the afternoon. Did P.T. at 2.45. Had a shower in evening. No water pressure, and consequently only a trickle. Lovely day. Sent P.C. home.

7 April. Went on the walk during the morning. Lovely day. Read in the afternoon. P.T. at 2.45. Wrote letter-card home. Did my laundry up.

8 April. Played soccer at 9.30 for an hour. Played 'back' and our side won 2-0. John drew my parcel including cocoa, good biscuits, a few sweets and the usual. Watched a soccer match. Went to draw lottery prize (pack of cards), but notice meant tomorrow at 4.00. Bought a spoon from canteen. Read during the day. Had some marsala. Put in for repatriation with John and C.B. I did some French in the afternoon. P.T. at 2.45. Sunny but a chilly wind.

9 April. French lessons at 9.00. 'Literature' at 9.45, dealing with 18th century drama – John Gay, Oliver Goldsmith and Richard Sheridan – and 18th century prose – Daniel Defoe, Addison and Steele, and Jonathan Swift. P.T. as usual in the afternoon. Finished reading *Catherine of Aragon* by Garrett Mattingley during the day. V. good book indeed. Got *Bengal Lancer* by F. Yeats-Brown out of library. Played 2 sets of tenniquoits in the evening. Sunny day – breeze.

10 April. Shave. Read in the morning. Lovely day. Played tenniquoits after 'tea' with Altree, 'Kiwi' and John. Had some marsala. Had quite a good shower in evening.

24

11 April. Did not wake up in time for Communion. Went to Matins. Lovely day. 'Words and Music' in the afternoon – songs with 4 banjoes, news, piano solo, talk on a N.Z. University Rugby team's tour of Japan (1931), cello solo, and 'Smuts' by De Villiers Graffe. Played a return tenniquoits match with John, Kiwi and Altree. We lost 2 sets – only just!! Went to the church services in the evening. Got a New Testament from Wiles who took the service. Read 2 old *Punch* numbers in evening.

12 April. Went before a British Medical Board in the morning. 114 had applied for repatriation!! Finished reading *Bengal Lancer* – good book in parts but dull where he describes the Hindu faith. Got *Prince Charlie* out of library. Drew tin of Ovaltine and 20 cigarettes out of 'Exchange' for cheese and cocoa, I put in on Friday. P.T. at 2.45 – harder table. Did some French for tomorrow's lesson. Read in the evening.

13 April. 'Literature' talk at 9.45 dealing with Swift and 18th century especially Burke. French lesson at 11.00. John drew my tin of condensed milk out of store for me. Finished reading *Prince Charlie* by Compton Mackenzie before P.T. at 2.45. Played single tenniquoits with John continuously from after roll call 5.00 until dinner and afterwards until 7.45. He won! Very strenuous! Had a good hot shower afterwards and then an excellent cup of Ovaltine. Then I wrote P.C. home. Read some more. Lovely day.

14 April. Went on walk. Lovely day. Too hot for walking. Did my French sentences when I got back. Played John tenniquoits after lunch until 2.00. Beat him! Went to lecture on 'Crete' by Lt Col Watson at 2.00. P.T. at 2.45. Read after 'tea'. Just finished *The Splendour of the Dawn* in time to get *The Bridge of San Luis Rey* out of library. The former was very good. Wrote letter-card home, Read in evening.

☆　☆　☆

22 April. Maundy Thursday. Slight rain during dull day. Read most of the time. My parcel day. Went to Evensong in the evening.

23 April. Good Friday. Hot-cross (Red X)!! buns for breakfast. Dull day again. Tried to go on the walk, but only 200 allowed. Over 300 were lined up and the first 200 only

partitioned off. However, about 20 extra tacked themselves on. When we got through the wire we were sent back!! Read in morning, after a walk at the end of the camp. Went to the last 2 hours of the '3 hours devotion' from 1.00-3.00. Read during rest of the day.

24 April. Foggy in early morning, so no walk. 1st day of Sports meeting – continued all day. 'Highlight' was in afternoon when C.B. ran in 3-mile race. Only 6 entries and C.B. came in 5th – one had dropped out! V. good performance – ran all the way!! Read a bit. Kiwi (Bob Beauchamp) and I played Charles Gatenby and Mac (Mackenzie Smith) at bridge in evening. We each won a rubber, but they won on points. A month since I had any mail. Dull day.

25 April. Easter Sunday. Went to H.C. at 7.00. Porridge for breakfast. Went to Matins at 10.00. (There were three communions and all were crowded.) Sunny and warm day. John and I played C.B. and Altree tenniquoits. Lost! Lunch – lettuce, spring onions, asparagus and cheese. Went to 'Words and Music' in the afternoon. The band played some marches, news as usual, violin solo by Len Inskip. Talk by Padre Birnie Allen on 'Some Easter Ceremonies at Jerusalem', the choir sang a few numbers, and Arthur Duvine gave a talk on organization of Scotland Yard. Went to the service with Olly in the evening. (Good dinner – steak and macaroni, peas, kidney beans, spuds and Xmas pudding.)

26 April. Sports finals. The band played on and off. 2 clowns put in appearance. The sun was out all the time and it was very pleasant. Phil Myers gave demonstration of how to run mile, and was beaten by 2 others in the mile in aft. All usual events. Gladiators 5th out of 8!! Played Tom Wallace tenniquoits after lunch. He won 1 set (6-4) but the last game went on over 10 minutes. Played tenniquoits with Padre Allen (?!) against Padre Burns and another. We won 2-1 sets (before dinner). After dinner, played with John against Phil and Ralph Noyes. We lost 2-1 sets. Played 2 more sets with Phil versus other 2, and drew 1-1. Played bridge with John v Phil and Noyes in evening. Won first set and were winning second – altogether 1700 up. Wrote diary for 2 days afterwards.

27 April. Col Page, Tsouchos and Massey. 'Literature' at 9.45 dealing with Wordsworth. No French today. John and I played Tom and Baker tenniquoits. Lost 3-0 sets. P.T. at 2.45. (Played Patience with John before). Lecture by Capt Franklin on 'Shakespeare and Elizabethan Box-Office' at 4.00. V. good. Kiwi and I played Charles and Mac at bridge. Won 2 rubbers, and were 1670 points up at the end. Wrote P.C. home.

28 April. Warm and sunny. Went on walk with Read in aft. Finished *Greece under the Romans* by George Finlay. V. good book but rather heavy. May read it a second time later on. Got *Lectures on Shakespeare* out of library. John and I played bridge with Phil and Capt – in evening. We won by 470 points after playing 2 rubbers, although we had lost the first rubber hopelessly. I got a 'grand slam' on the 3 no-trump contract once!! Lights went out about 10.00 – air raid?

29 April. Roll call 7.00. Wrote letter-card home. Drew a N.Z. parcel. Shared it with John's English parcel to get variety. Went to lecture after lunch by Duvine on Organization of districts in London (of the police), and various crimes. Went to lecture at 4.00 by Capt Franklin on 'Sir John Falstaff, a Study of Sensuality'. V. good. Read after roll call, and in evening. Dull and rainy day.

30 April. Roll call 7.00. Literature lecture on 'S.T. Coleridge'. French lessons at 11.30 when sentences were handed back and we did some dictation. Got a letter from Margie addressed to Altamura – no postmark, envelope open, no letter and 4 snaps. Nothing much in aft. Lecture by Capt Franklin at 4.00 – 'Shakespeare Drama – a critical analysis'. Had some vino in evening. John and I played Kiwi and Ken Altree at bridge in evening. We lost by 770 – our first defeat!! We both played badly! Warm day.

1 May. Sunny and warm day. Read in morning. Sat out in sun most of day – reading. Finished *Lectures on Shakespeare* by Coleridge, but had not read the whole of it. V. good but heavy. Got *The Face in the Night* by Edgar Wallace out of library. No 'showers' at night for some reason. 5 weeks since I had a letter.

☆　☆　☆

3 May. Rained all day. Read most of the time. Finished *The Face in the Night*. Excellent book. Started reading *Notre Dame* by

Victor Hugo. Went to a lecture in the morning by Padre Wiles – 'Psychology, Morality and Religion.' Went to the 'News' review by Dimbleby in the afternoon. Read most of the day.

☆　☆　☆

8 May. Scrambled eggs for breakfast. Read most of day. Finished *Notre Dame*. V. good book after I had got into it. The first part rather drawn-out and dull. John and I beat Mac and Kiwi at bridge in evening. We played nearly 3 rubbers and were about 550 points up at the end, after winning first rubber without them scoring a point! Fall of Tunis and Bizerta. Library.

9 May. Went to Communion at 7.15. Dozed for an hour after breakfast. Was late going to Matins (during first hymn). 'Words and Music' in aft. – Dance band, 'Dimbleby', and talks on Fiji Islands and S.A. law. Italian 'Empire' Day! Went to the service in evening – taken by Birnie Allen. Crowded. Just got a seat at back with Olly.

10 May. Orderly Officer. Got up at 7.10 and took names of 'sick'. Lecture on 'Psychology, Morality and Religion' – final talk in series by Padre Wiles. 'Parcel fatigue'. Had my hair cut. Read most of afternoon. Kiwi and I played bridge with Mac and Charles in evening. We lost by 850 points – nearly 2 rubbers played. No cards! Went round black-out at night.

11 May. Sunny day. Read most of day. Vatican Xmas message arrived. On parcel list for tomorrow. Wrote P.C. home – and also reply to Vatican message.

12 May. Collected my parcel of 500 cigs from Garpa. Read. John and I lost to Jim and Don at tenniquoits (2-1 sets) in aft. P.T. at 2.45. Finished my French which I started in morning. Kiwi and I played bridge with Mac and Charles in evening. About 1,800 points down in 2 rubbers!! Started letter-card home (in print). Warm day.

13 May. Laundry day. Wrote letter-card home (300 words in print). Drew a parcel (British) – a 'Private's Parcel'!! John and I lost 3-0 sets at tenniquoits to Jim and Don. Then Don and I took the other 2 on, and just lost by 10-8 games (1 set). Read most of aft. Finished *Sir Philip Sidney* by H. R. Fox-Bourne. V. good book. P.T. at 2.45. Got *St Joan of Arc* by V.

Sackville-West out of library. Kiwi and I played Mac and Charles at bridge and won by 40 in 2 rubbers (one each) after being over 1,000 down at 'half time'. I got a small no-trump slam in last hand! Hot day.

14 May. Went to literature – dealing with Lord Byron. Went through some geometry with Don!! Forgot about French! Read in aft. P.T. at 2.45. C.B. and I played 2 N.Z.s bridge in even. After being well over 1,000 down at 'hot water' time we picked up and were only 500 down at end – C.B. got a '7 hearts' and I got a 4 no-trumps – and we finished off with a 3 no-trump hand. V. enjoyable – good hands.

15 May. O.R.'s sports meeting. I went on the walk – hot day. Only about 33 went. V. pleasant. P.T. at 2.45. John and I beat Jim and Don 2-1 sets tenniquoits in aft. Read. C.B. and I played 2 N.Z.s bridge in evening. Lost again!! About 1,600 points down. V. enjoyable. Hot day.

16 May. Went to Communion at 8.15. Matins at 10.00. Read afterwards. 'Words and Music' in aft. – Trumpet solo, talk on S.A. Railways (Sarah), violin solo, news, 2 saxophones and trumpet trio (Temptation Rag and Bugle Call Rag beginning with It. 'Changing the Guard' call!!), and talk on a 'Springbok' Rugger visit to Argentina. Hot day. John and I played Jim and Don tenniquoits after roll call. We lost 2-1 sets, but won on games and played 2 sets with sun in our eyes!! Went to church in evening. Read.

17 May. Read most of morn and aft. P.T. at 2.45. C.B. and I played 2 N.Z.s bridge in evening. We won by about 1,700 points. V. enjoyable. Windy and sunny.

18 May. Literature dealing with drama and poetry of Victorian period – incl. Wilde, Tennyson and Browning, briefly. French at 11.30. Lovely day. Finished my book in the afternoon (*Joan of Arc*) v. good. Got *I Will Repay* by Orczy out of library. P.T. at 2.45. C.B. and I played 2 N.Z.s (incl. Mick and Maori) bridge in even. We lost by 2,800 points, but they had the cards and we had some bad luck! They were v. good players.

19 May. Wrote P.C. home. Read most of day. Lovely day. P.T. at 2.45. Did French in aft. Played with a N.Z. against Bettison and a N.Z. at bridge in even. We won by 1,250 points. I got a grand slam but only called 3 no-trumps once.

20 May. Had scrambled eggs (flakes) for breakfast. Lovely day. Wrote L/C home. Drew parcel. Read most of day. Finished *I Will Repay'* by Orczy – v. good book. Got *The English Countryman* by H.J. Massingham out of library. P.T. at 2.45. Nothing else special.

21 May. Literature dealing mostly with the Pre-Raphaelites, and the prose of 19th century. No French – but had homework returned. Read. P.T. at 2.45. Went to a lecture by Capt Houghton on 'Population Problems' – v. good – at 4.00. Went for a walk round camp in even. and went to bed early.

22 May. Daddy's birthday. Went to an 'Economics' lecture at 9.45 by Capt Houghton dealing with Britain's and other country's economic history after last war. V. good. Too late for walk at 10.30. Read during the day. P.T. Went to 'Robin Hood' in evening. Excellent show – Ken Altree played part of 'Penelope' (v.g.). Orchestral music could have been lighter. Thunderstorm in late aft. Marsala.

☆ ☆ ☆

24 May. Went on the walk at 10.00. Given bunch of wild roses by a little girl!! V. warm and sunny for the most part. Had diarrhoea! Read a bit. Played 'back' at soccer at 4.00. We won 2-0!! (Practice Gladiators game). P.T. at 2.45. Roll call at 6.00 from now on. Had a 'bucket' swill down. Changed 'sittings' with Bob for dinner. Made questionnaire out re mail etc. Took Salts at night.

25 May. Camp Orderly Officer. Roll call at 7.30 from now on! Got up at 6.30. Spent most of day running about the camp for the Adjutant and sitting in Orderly Room. Our wing (SA) was washed out and so we had to move our beds out. Could not go to literature or French lessons. Diarrhoea no better. Finished my book. Very interesting, and last chapter particularly good. *The English Countryman* was really the history of the peasants, labourers, craftsmen, yeomen, squires, parsons etc. Got *St Francis of Assissi* by G.K. Chesterton out of library. No P.T. Mac and I played 2 N.Z.s at bridge in evening. We lost by about 1,700 points. Went round camp 'blackouts' afterwards. Windy day with dust blowing about.

26 May. Mummy's birthday. Got up just after 6.00. Had a hot shower after the Italians before roll call. Reported sick at

8.30. Given salts and some green stuff to drink and 4 tablets (bismuth?) for tonight and in morning. Wrote P.C. home. Diarrhoea no better. Did not eat much. Did not go to P.T. as a result. Finished reading *St Francis of Assissi* – v. interesting but v. sketchy book. Got *Down the Garden Path* by Beverley Nichols out of library. Had a letter dated 26 April from home – first from Mummy since 27 Nov (dated 21 Jan) – addressed straight here, No 26 and I have only had 7 incl. a P.C. News that playing fields being ploughed up partly for potatoes. Hopes of early release. Needless to say – letter extremely welcome. Wrote letter-card home (288 words) in print.

27 May. Did laundry up. Drew N.Z. parcel (incl. tin cheese, jam, honey, butter, coffee with milk and emergency ration). 2 N.Z.s bridge (incl. Peter) in even. C.B. was my partner. We won by 500 points – not v. good cards. Strawberries and cream for dinner!!

☆　☆　☆

4 June. Went on the walk with Mick (Michael) at 9.30. V. enjoyable. French afterwards. Finished reading *King Arthur* in aft. V. good book although written in rather old English. Got *Confessions of a Young Man* by George Moore out of library. P.T. as usual. Went to lecture on 'Prehistoric Man' at 4.00. Dozed off towards end!! Played bridge in even. C.B. and I lost to Peter and Tony Jacobs (N.Z.) by 450 points, but they just had better cards.

5 June. Went to Economics lecture in morn. Read most of day. P.T. in aft. Good lecture on 'Initial Landings in Tunisia' at 8.00. Had 5 letters in even!!

6 June. Went to Communion. Roll call at 8.00 again. Matins (by Padre Laurence, a new arrival) at 9.45. Finished reading *Confessions of a Young Man* and did not agree with any of it. Got *Across Iceland* by Olive Murray Chapman out of library. Went to church – v. good – in even. Musical Society Concert afterwards. Words and Music in aft. Not as good as usual – cello solo, piano solo, song (solo), news, talk on yachting (could not hear it!!) and talk by Francis Penly on 'Cotswolds' (v.g.) incl. piano solos, piano and violin and songs – classical. V. good.

7 June. Nothing special. Read – finished *Across Iceland* – v.

good book (although 1929 edition). P.T. in aft. John and Don started 'boot-black shop' – 2 Lire a pair!! Did French in even.

8 June. Got *Ariel* (The Life of Shelley) by André Maurois out of library. French lesson. Heard that Peter Tivey (Australian) had died at Altamura at beginning of April. 4 letters from home (3 from Mum, dated 15 Feb/No 13, Feb 11/No 12 and Apr 10/No 23), and 1 from D. dated 10 Apr. News that all prisoners in Hong Kong complete, but Teddy not amongst them. P.T. as usual. John and I were going to a soccer practice, but they were late starting, so we did not bother!! C.B. and I lost by 500 points to Peter and Tony Jacobs in even. V. poor cards of which we got the worse.

9 June. Wrote P.C. home and most of L/C in print. Read during day. P.T. in aft. Lecture No 2 of Tunisian campaign at 4.15. Meeting of French Society at 8.15 – just to state the future programme.

10 June. Finished *Ariel* – v.g. book. Handed boots in for repair. Laundry. Got *The Young Melbourne* by David Cecil out of library. Did French translation after lunch. P.T. Read in even. (Parcels in morn. John and I shared Eng and N.Z.)

11 June. Went on the walk with Bob. French afterwards. Dozed in aft. Missed P.T. Read a bit. Went to 'On the Spot' in even. – Edgar Wallace's play given by the ORs with Rex Kirk in it. V. good indeed.

12 June. Read most of day. Finished *The Young Melbourne* (v.g.). Got *Elizabethan Commentary* by Hilaire Belloc out of library. Had some marsala. Bob and I played Ken Alltree and a N.Z. bridge in even. We won by 1,170 points. (I got a Grand Slam and Bob got a small one – but we did not call them as in both cases Bob's hand did not merit going on. Pantellaria fell.

☆ ☆ ☆

21 June. Booked the barbers for tomorrow week at 4.15. Did my French. Read. P.T. in aft. Borrowed *How Green Was My Valley* by Richard Llewellyn from C.B. 'French Circle' at 3.45 – Idioms. Played baseball for my room in even. V. amusing game. 2 or 3 hundred watched and were well entertained!! We lost by about 16-14 (?) to room 5A4. I scored 1 run! V.

enjoyable.

22 June. Our wing washed out. Moved beds out. John and I played soccer in a 'friendly game' for Glads. v Head Hunters. We won 3-1. I scored a goal!! – off shoulder from a corner! Was playing left wing. V. warm. French afterwards. Lost my cup and teaspoon outside before moving beds in. Read in aft. Had issue of Vermouth. Went to 'Psychology' lecture on 'Reproduction' in even. Read.

23 June. Wrote P.C. Read most of day. P.T. in aft. Lecture on 46 Div in Tunis at 4.15. Nothing else special.

24 June. Wrote letter-card home (282). Hot as ever. Finished *How Green Was My Valley*. After being disappointed at first, I thoroughly enjoyed it. Did my French in afternoon. Played baseball for 5A1 in even. Had to stop before finished as a soccer match had to be played. I caught someone out in the outfield!!

27 June. Went to Communion. Got *Victoria Regina* by Laurence Housman out of library. Watched England v. Scotland soccer match. Drew 0-0. Went to Art Gallery with Bob in aft. Some excellent paintings. Also v. good but few 'crafts'. 'Words and Music' at 4.00. Piano solo (v.g.) 'Canada', concertina, news, 3 saxophones and clarinet (?), 'Brigade of Guards' (V.G. speaker). Went with Olly to church (Rodger). Musical Society Show at 9.00 v. good, including 3 dances of Edward German. Cooler.

28 June. Read all day. Finished *Victoria Regina*. V. amusing play. French Society – *Menage à Trois* by Pousson. V. amusing, as usual! Warm again but not unbearable.

4 July. Did not wake up to go to Communion. John, Don and I had scrambled eggs and potatoes for breakfast. Went to Matins. Took *S. Africa* back to library. Read *English Women* by Edith Sitwell. Letter No 27 (d May 4) from Mummy. News that school being put on 'mains' as water 'still' undrinkable. Also that 130 boys now at school (and 1 maid!). Went to church in even. (Padre Watson N.Z.) 'Musical Society' . V. hot weather started again, after cooler 'break'.

5 July. Walk in morning – was not on it! Extra roll call during morning. Phil Myers and I drew 1-1 with Bob and Don at tenniquoits in aft. We won first set and then my feet became sore so I could not run about!! Several blisters on account of v. hot ground!! Had shower afterwards. 'Introductory' lecture to 'Political Theory' series by Bonham-Carter. V. good (11.45). Went to the play reading society in even. The cast read out Sheridan's *The Rivals*. V. amusing, but a lot had to be missed out. Peach season.

6 July. *'Americana Propaganda Novel'* by Emery at 11.00 in series of literature. Beginner's Italian afterwards. Bob and I went 'Pronunciation'. C.B. and I (the Queen's Regt.) took John and Don (RAF) at tenniquoits in aft. We just won 2-1 sets after very close match. We won last set 7-5. V. enjoyable. Shower afterwards. Had some marsala in even. Phil and I beat Trevor Atchley and Gordon Rowlandson at bridge in even, by 1,700 points. A South African in Bungalow 6 died from a heart attack during the night. (No games tomorrow).

☆　☆　☆

10 July. Learnt Italian with Bob from 11.00 until 4.30 in aft!! Phil Myers and I played Trevor and Dick Bettison bridge in even. We won by 780 points. News that we attacked Sicily last night.

11 July. Went to Communion at 7.15. Matins. Read a bit in aft. 'Words and Music' – 'Ragamuffins' playing 'White Christmas', 'How Green Was My Valley' and 'The Song of the Isles' amongst other things, also piano medley; talk on the 'Shop' (Woolwich) v.g., news and v.g talk on 'Debunking the Bunk-house' (Canadian ranching) by Padre Lawrence. Went to church in even. Musical Society afterwards.

12 July. Did a lot of Italian with Bob in morn and aft. Also read a bit. Lecture on 'Law and the State' at 11.45. C.B. and I beat Bettison and Cox by 1,480 points at bridge in even.

13 July. French at 9.30. Bob and I did Italian after literature (American Social Novel). Read in aft and did more Italian. Phil and I played Trevor and Mac at bridge in even. We drew! Only 30 difference.

14 July. Wrote P.C. home. Did Italian with Bob most of the day. Read a bit. Phil and I drew with Mac and Bettison in even. (bridge). 20 points up! Letter (No 24 d. Apr 17) from Mummy.

19 July. Did some Italian with Bob. Poor talk on 'Political Thought in Middle Ages'. More Italian in aft. Finished reading *Henry VIII* (at last!). Quite interesting, but rather 'heavy'. Phil and I played Trevor and Mac at bridge in even. Lost by 1,400 points. Had awful cards (only played 2 hands), but got them 'down' a lot at beginning. Letter d. 27 June from Margie. News that my P.C. to her took nearly 6 months!! Got *The Queen's Cause* out of library. (About Mary Q of Scots – by Mrs H. Barclay).

☆ ☆ ☆

24 July. Went to Intermediate Italian class with Olly. (One chap gave short talk on visit to Cologne from London. Had to read and translate a piece out of 'Sapere', but managed it all right!!) A.R.A. overhead! News that west part of Sicily incl. Palermo evacuated. No mail still!! – all beginning of alphabet!! Read in aft. Boxing, wrestling, Jujitsu and balancing performance in even. Band in attendance. Commandant watched. Balancing and wrestling best. C.B. was M.C.

25 July. Matins. (A.R.A.) Did more Italian (Bob still busy in theatre). Read a bit in aft. 'Words and Music' was exceptionally good. Camp orchestra (Patrick Quirke) played March from 'Robin Hood', and 'Poet and Peasant' amongst other tunes. News, and talk by Arthur Duveen on 'American Journey in 1941' – military mission – v.g. indeed. Musical society in even.

26 July. News that Marshal Badoglio had ousted Mussolini. Arthur (D) and I played John and Don at tenniquoits in morn. We lost 3-0 but put up a good fight!! 1st time A had played for 10 years! A.R.A. 3 letters and 5 snaps from M., and Italians hoisted Royalist flag and saluted it. Read more of book on Mary Queen of Scots. Too heavy. Took it back – unfinished. Got *A Thatched Roof* by Beverley Nichols out of library. Phil and I beat Mac and Trevor by 630 points at bridge. Letter No 30 (23 May) from M.

☆ ☆ ☆

30 July. Papers no longer allowed in POW camps by order of Italian Gen Staff. French at 9.30 before which I did a bit of translation with 'Humph'. Arthur (D) and I played Noyes and Don tenniquoits after morning 'tea'. We lost!! Had 'bath' after 'quoits. Finished reading *A Thatched Roof* in aft. Very enjoyable, but not quite as good as *Down Garden Path*. Got Bev. Nichols's *Prelude* from library. Did a lot of Italian on my own in aft. Mac and Trevor v Phil and me at bridge in even. We had not many cards, but I finished up with a small slam in spades (double, re-doubled) getting 7, and being 360 points up at end. Managed to throw away best losers else I should have only have got 6. (Mills 'Gremlin' went to Hosp – jaundice).

☆ ☆ ☆

2 August. Finished reading *Prelude* – v. good. Arthur and I played tenniquoits. He won by 2-0, but very even games. Went to lecture by Bonham-Carter on 'Conservatism'. V. good. V. hot day again. Learnt up to end of Lesson 18 in Italian in aft. Got *The Good Companions* (Vol I) by J.B.P. out of library. French society at 4.00 pm – Quillan gave talk on S.E. Coast of France. News that Ites in S. laid down their arms (?) Did some Italian in even. – Olly marked 2 of my It. exercises. Read.
    3 August. Read. Played Arthur 'quoits. Lost 2-1 sets – 6-5, 4-6, 6-4 to him. V. even and energetic! Had 'bath' afterwards. Read in aft. Phil and I v Mac and Trevor at bridge. We lost by 1,030 points, won first and last rubber (700s) and did not win another game otherwise – no cards.

☆ ☆ ☆

6 August. French at 9.30. (list of Fr. 'Dishes' etc.) Economic lecture at 11.45. Finished reading *The Warden*. V. good. Got *Good Companions* (Vol II) from library. News that Orel has fallen, and 'reports' that Catania has gone. Read in aft. Went to French Society in evening. Busson gave talk on Paris – too fast!!

22 August. Communion. Matins. Got *Life Among the English* by Rose Macauley from library. V. interesting short history of the life lived by all classes since before invasion by Romans. Played 'quoits with Arthur. He won 2-1. Very even games. 21st birthday of 'Words and Music'. Exceptionally good programme incl. choir, orchestra, ('Washington Post' among other tunes), dance band, soloists, news and v.g. talk on 'Tribal Customs of the Scot' (!!) by MacQuarrie. Church and Musical Society in even. Kharkov fell.

27 August. News that Graham Boyton and Sprake were being repatriated tomorrow (loss of limbs scheme). French in morn. (Battle of Hastings account read out to us). 'World Economy' lecture. V. good. Read in aft. Copied out verbs of avere, essere, parlare and temere. Went to French Society in even. *(Lettres de Mon Moulin* – Daudet).

31 August. Sat in the sun before 'morning tea' and read. Inoculated at 11.15. Read most of the day, finished short book on Scotland (v. interesting). John and I lost 2-1 sets of quoits to Penley and Don. I should not really have played – being inoculated this morning. Felt a little 'shivery' in even. but not much.

4 September. V. heavy rain. Italian (Inter) – we each had to talk but it did not come round to me. Read. Talked with Tongue before aft. roll call. Beer issue, About 15 new arrivals came incl. 3 Americans.

8 September. Ital (Inter) – Conversation; I spoke for a few minutes on the Russian Front!! Played Arthur 'quoits. Lost 2-0 before A.R.A. V. even games. Read in aft. Wrote L/C to Mrs Sharp and home. Armistice proclaimed by Marshal Badoglio at 7.00 pm!! Was watching football match when we all rushed to gate to hear news. Ites kissing each other. Sing song with dance band in even. Free issue of marsala. Camp gone mad!! Impressive rendering of 'God Save the King' when all, incl. 2 It. sentries and those drunk, stood to attention. Roll call in even.

9 September. Porridge, bacon and sausages for breakfast. News that Bologna, Modena and Capri (?) commands been occupied by Germans. Thought that they are securing L of C. Thanksgiving church service in Bungalow 6 yard. Big crowd. Drew parcel (Canadian). Was Bung. ord. off. Had to get up early but did nothing else! The Italians gradually and then suddenly filtered homewards with suitcases!! About less than 100 of our chaps went off, but most did not go as S.B.O. had told us to remain for orders. Camp left unguarded. S.B.O. then told us that we could go if we wanted but he advised us not to. Then, before he had finished speaking, the Jerries arrived! (An officer and 1 OR had previously been to look at camp). News that Naples, Genoa and Livorno had had landings by our troops. Not true. Good meals. Got everything out of store. Day of anticlimax, waiting and suspense. Got things ready for possible sudden departure. Gen opinion that very unlikely that we would go to Germany. Sentries (G) not communicative. More Gs arrived in even. England beat N. Zealand 3-1 soccer. None of our planes over all day. Several enemy ones. One dropped signal in even – 3 red and 1 white lights. Periodical firing all round camp during day. It Officers taken away under arrest (?) Ital padre said goodbye to RC padre. No bread in camp today!! No aft. papers. How can we get news without Ite sentries? Contrast in people's faces with last night! All wondering if it would have been better to have gone. A few who got away were brought back by Jerries. Machine gun from in Bungalow. Pamphlet calling on Ites to rally into German Army dropped into camp. 3 lots of Germans have already guarded us. 2 escaped during night.

10 September. Stayed in bed quite late. John and Don cooked 2 tins of eggs. Good feed. Nothing much going on. A few It. Offrs staying as administrators. Don't come into camp. A Sikh came in for Red X parcels for another camp – short of food. Our rations came in. Holes made in roof (for hiding). (Germans found these out – no good now.) Got *Rebecca* by D. Du Maurier out of library. Got all food out of store. My birthday and I did not realize it till tomorrow. Alf Adams caught by sentry under rubbish dump. Dance band performance in aft. Read in even. Long nominal roll call by Germans in even.

11 September. Stayed in bed till 10.00. News to move!! This aft or tomorrow. Packed up. Burnt practically all clothing etc. and food (spare), as we could only take what we could carry. Olly went to hospital. Got pay sheets from bank. Store thrown open for any food we wanted. Drew Red X parcel. 120 cigs issued out. to each man. Big bonfires – tins of food banging. A lot given to It. civilians (ie thrown over the walls). Great commotions and depression. Looked for hiding place – none good enough. Rumours galore. David Dale (Adjt) went out. G. Area Commandant knew nothing of move!! Suggested 100 at a time going to a swimming bath!!! Order given not to burn clothing and food. Drew plate and fork from Mess. Walked round camp most of day. Saw Olly in hospital. Ites talking to us from outside. Trains almost at a standstill. No transport to take us!! Another respite. News that Alpini fighting near Brenner. Our troops occupied south almost to Rome (?) Partially unpacked in even!! Recces.!

12 September. (Sun) Got up after 3.00 am. News to move for groups 1,2,3,4,5,6,7,8,10,12 – lucky ones were 5,9,11. I was in 9!! But the 1st 5 on list of No 9 had to do runner duty for Ord. Room (Phil, Geoff Dunn, John, Don and I). Had tea and bit of meat roll. We got groups in correct order to move off carrying kit. Watched them move out – poor beggars. V. loaded up. Moved over to Bungalow 4 (a.10) afterwards. Then breakfast – which I thought was lunch!! Rumours of landings at Livorno, Albania and France (definitely). This proved to be untrue (18/Sept/43)!!! Schemes galore. Tidied up books, food (unopened), clothing, beds, chairs etc. 2 kids were hurt in Modena when they were playing with a German grenade. Both brought into camp hospital. One thought certain to die. Later taken to Modena Hospital. Relations came into camp to see them. (President of French Society, Simpson – went out

with them dressed as a civilian!) Service in evening – Padre K
Watson and YMCA man took it. About 250 left in camp. Air
activity. 3 tried to get over wall. Shot. One brought back. 2 got
away. V. hot weather.

13 September. Cleaned room out. Hot day. Wireless across
wire. Groups 5 and 11 went at 4.00 in trucks, but we all had to
prepare. Most of Group 9 had to go to make up numbers. I
was lucky again!! They took Red X stuff – in separate trucks!!
Still tons here. Ate a lot!! I with John, Don, C.B. etc. still here –
47 offrs besides ones at hospital (Olly incl.) Got some pudding
from Red X store. Roll call with kit. Moved to Bungalow 3
(B10). Took kit. Not allowed out. Had good feed of Red X
food. Birnie Young found under tomatoes!! (by Germans)

14 September. Orders to move at 8.45. Did not go till lunch
time. Made several brews of tea before we set off. Hospital
moved on mattresses (some of them!!) (Roof, double doors,
ground, water-tanks, step to kitchen, sewer – places to hide.)
Unlucky to be confined to Bungalow 5!! Moved in trucks with
quite a number of invalid parcels. Great farewell from
civilians (V-sign). Pleasant journey via Reggio Emilia to
Mantua (Mantova) football ground and cycling stadium. Got
grapes at a halt on the way. Pontoon-bridge over PO. C.B. and
I made shelter of blankets. Brewed tea rather unsuccessfully!!
John and 'Humph' gave me a drink later on. Slept on and off
(hard and cold!!). (Bread issue.)

15 September. Brewed up on Hutt's fire. Parade at 10.15.
Olly acting as interpreter – Geoff Dunn who had been
interpreter was not feeling well. Lt Col Webb (N.Z.) handed
parade over to Sgt Major with smart salute! Moved at 11.00.
Suitcase too heavy so jettisoned some of food, as we had to
walk!! 'Chain' of men to get invalid parcels to gate. Some went
on 1 of 2 (or 3) trucks for hospital patients. Others?? Dreadful
walk to station (2 kilo). Gave a lot of food to civilians outside
camp. We were under the charge of a Sgt Major – a 'lovely' (ie
the opposite) man! I carried suitcase first, then changed over
with C.B. for his kit-bag. He soon staggered (!!) and I took over
till an Ite boy took it on his cycle. All civilians were kind and
eager to help. John Heslop almost escaped by merging with
civilians. Got suitcase back just before the station. Cattle-
trucks. C.B. John Heslop (N.Z.), Birnie Young (N.Z.), Evan
Wilson (N.Z.) in carriage amongst others (10). Ite civilians very

generous – water, lemonade, a little vino, grapes, cigarettes, bread (which we refused), etc. Talked to a few railway officials and others. A German officer spoke to us in v. good English. (He had been in India and Nigeria besides England.) Most of the train was taken up by Italian officer POWs, and some Yugoslavs. We greeted them. Most of Italian women were crying (all along the journey). 100 per cent for us. Spoke to many. Set off in aft. Reached Verona in daylight.

16 September. Unscrewed window and undid back door. After dark the train was travelling too fast to do a jump, but it eventually slowed down. (Evan W, John H, and then C.B. Evan fell badly.) Train stopped for four hours halt. Birnie Young v. annoyed as Jim had got in the way and had funked it!! George Walker, myself and a S.A. were after Birnie. I did not sleep because of waiting. V. tired. Train started, but door would not open as next carriage's step had jammed it. However, train stopped in few minutes and daylight came. The mist would not thicken! (We had passed through Padua during the night?) Pretty scenery in day when we were approaching mountains. Went through Treviso, Udine (Roll call etc!). Guard on opened doors now!! Near the frontier we were removed to OR's truck only 7 of us now. 19 in OR's truck. (Glasses knocked off!!! Ribs hit – rough treatment by German guards.) Birnie was taken for an Ite but Trevor (in our truck) unfortunately spoke to him. V. little room in OR's truck. A train-load of Ite OR's joined us there – packed in open trucks. Gave them food, tobacco and clothing. V. grateful. We moved v. slowly. No water and not allowed out because of escapes! A new guard (Austrian) came on at Villach and we had a 'rear' (well wanted!), filled water-bottles and had bread and polony issued. I had slept very little owing to there being no room to lie down. Birnie Young took a goods-train the other way.

17 September. Arrived in morning at Spittal-am-Drav (36 kilos from Villach by road). Walked mile to camp with kit. V. welcome shower. Had clothing disinfected. Moved into room with Phil Myers, Don Hutt, John Mills, Humph, Francis Penley, Geoff Dunne and Pat McCambridge amongst others (14 in all). Had some potato soup. V. good. 1st hot 'eatable' since Monday morning. Margarine, bread, sugar and tea (Red X) issue to rooms. Serbs and French and Russians at camp besides British NCOs. Recent influx of 1000s of all ranks from Italy. Olly and I spoke to some French and Russians. Got bed ready, cleaned room out, and 'brewed up'. Put anti-lice powder over floor, blanket etc. Borrowed blanket from S.A. Only a small amount of kit as we could only take what we could carry. Another lot of potato soup in even. Roll call in aft. Slept v. well, but v. hard on bed boards. Listened to the Russians singing.

18 September. Lt Col Page was at the camp from Camp No 5. Roll call at 8.00. Walked round with Olly and Geoff in morn. Washing by Russians. Filled diary in during afternoon. 5 more came into room. Got washing back in even. V. well done indeed (gave biscuits). Heard part of Fr. concert with Olly. Also listened to R's singing. Phil and I played bridge with Pat and John. We just won. Better sleep – although I had diarrhoea (black bread?). Wrote P.C. home (in Cpl's name).

19 September. Roll call at 9.00. Brewed up afterwards. Read Daphne Du Maurier's *Come Wind, Come Weather*. Quite good. Also continued reading her *Rebecca*. Potato soup at 12.00. Watched some good soccer in even.

20 September. Olly went to hospital (diarrhoea). We washed the room out – 4 from each end. I drew unlucky! The sun went in and it started to rain when we had almost finished. V. heavy rain and v. cold from then on. Read in aft. Potato soup at 1.00. SBO's roll call parade (extra one) at 4.00. Could not play bridge in even. as the light was too bad, so we talked. Very cold night – only one thin blanket on bed boards. Got the 'blackout' down in night to put on my bed!! (Snow on mountains).

21 September. Sunny day, but cold early. Potato soup at 11.15. Withdrew tins (Red X) from store, as we are moving tomorrow. Sat in the sun. Brewed a cup of tea outside after lunch. Watched soccer in evening: England 3 – Scotland 4. We were winning 2-0 at one time. Good game. (Started packing in aft.) Good meal of Red X meats in evening. Also pudding from parcel. Phil and I beat Blackie (Capt Blackwell) and Lt Col Henderson by 1,260 points at bridge – interrupted by lights going out for hour. Warmer night. Slept better. 'Canary' (ie secret wireless news) as usual in evening.

22 September. Packed. Had a few brews of tea, and some

potato soup. Marched out with all kit about 11.30. Went to field over the road for a search. Put heavy kit on truck, and marched down to station. 42 in each cattle truck – 41 in ours. Got in about 1.00 pm. Given bread and good cheese for journey – Penk, Vallitz, Böchstein, Rosenheim (early morn.). V. little room to sit down, lying down was out of the question. Stood up most of night, as I had a dreadful stomach ache. No water for nearly 24 hours (except 2 sips tomorrow morning and a few raindrops at night). Did not sleep for a second. Concentrated on saving 'No 2' till we were let out!!

23 September. Stopped at Landshut and went to lavatory. Our truck was just behind the 'WC' so we were not let out till 10 mins after the others. V. hurried when we did get out. Got limited supply of water in. We had bypassed Munich. Next stop was Regensburg where we were given some (rye?) soup. V. welcome but could get no water and could not go to lav. Passed through Schwartzburg and Wassan. Great difficulty and 'shut in' feeling with diarrhoea. Before dark I had to do it into a tin in Red X box, but no hole to throw it out of truck, so I kept it closed!! Somehow (I don't know how!) I managed not to go again during night. I even slept a bit – almost doubled-up.

24 September. Went through Riesa, Röderan and stopped at Neurburxdorf for over an hour. Eventually, we got out and this was our destination. Put heavy kit on some carts. Marched in jerks up to Stalag IV B* (near Burxdorf). Had a 'rear' in potato field on way (before we were 'shooed' off). Attempted escape on cycle. Just before we got to camp 'they' realized that we (officers) should not be there. The 2,000 (nearly) ORs went on into the camp. Water was brought out to us by the Russians and we went to the 'lav'. Pleasant weather. Eventually told we had to put up at this camp for time being. Pushed kit on carts up to entrance. Had a lovely hot shower and put all kit except food and tobacco through 'disinfestation'. We were inoculated for typhus and vaccinated afterwards. I was in first batch.

MUHLBERG STALAG IV B. This covered a huge area and contained tens of thousands of Russians, Indians, Poles, French etc. plus 300 British Officers (ie us), cramped into one hut with one wash basin and one or two lavatories. We could move about to the other nationalities and there was even a 'pub' there. However, food was v. short although we were allowed out on 'parole' walks and occasionally stole a few potatoes from the fields.

We then marched along to be searched. Handed 8 unopened tins into store (3 jam, 1 oats, 1 marg, 2 milk and 1 egg flakes). Then we were marched to our billets, but went the wrong way, and had to march all the way back again, with all our kit!! (Had stomach ache again as well!) Saw some RAF Sgts on our route. Eventually got to our hut. 3-tiered beds with palliasses and 2 blankets issued. Crowded room (189). 1 WC! and 1 wash-bowl (opened some showers tomorrow). Not allowed out of bungalow. Had some bread and sausage meat (tasteless!). Went to bed v. early after roll call. Had a very good night's sleep – the best since Modena.

25 September. Had some luke-warm Ovaltine about 7.00. Got up about 8.45. Shaved etc. Walk at 9.15 about a mile each way. Stayed hour at a depot. Turnip 'skilly' at lunch time. Filled diary in. 'Walk' again in aft. Stayed 1 hours at stores compound. Pleasant weather. Phil and I played Francis and Dick (H) bridge in even. We were 110 points down.

26 September. Went to Communion at 7.00 in the room (ie the one big sleeping room of the hut). Finished reading *Rebecca* during the day. V. good book. Did not go on morn walk – too cold a day. Potatoes for lunch. Phil and I played Bert Steele and Dick H bridge in aft. After being over 2,000 down at one time, we got 2 slams in one rubber and then had better cards than we had had before. We finished 2,640 points up. V. interesting (but not good!) bridge. Went for a walk around the camp with German under-officer. Saw some of our ORs – mostly Sgts in RAF (one had been on leave in London 8 days ago!!) Cold but refreshing walk. Church service in even in the room. Cold night.

☆ ☆ ☆

29 September. Went for a shower at 11.00. Nice and hot. Took some dirty washing and washed it in tubs provided. A lot of Ites outside waiting – recently come from Greece. Long walk in afternoon – past station, through Neuburxdorf and Burxdorf. Played bridge in even. Phil and I beat Blackie and partner by 650 points (about). Made 3 slams uncalled, and went down on 2 slams which we called (incl 7 no-trumps)!! Made some tea. (In the aft. walk we stopped at a cemetery where a lot of POWs incl. some British had been buried.

44

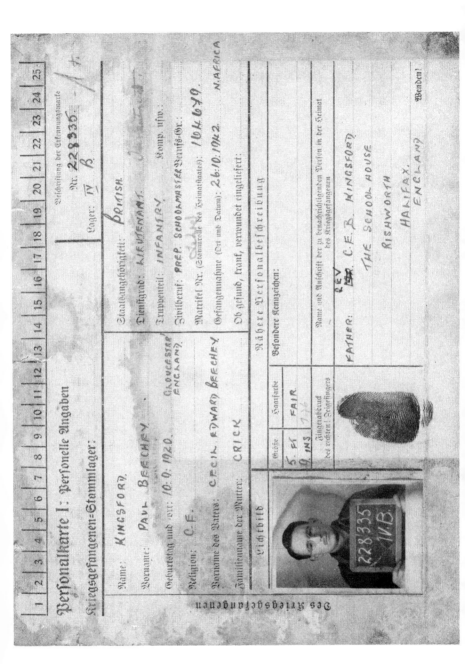

POW Identity Card

45

Communal grave for Rs under patch of grass – 100s.

2 October. Stayed in bed with cold all day. Read a bit of one of Olly's French books in aft. Had 2 aspirins and another pill. Nothing special. 14 or so new arrivals incl. a S.A. Dr from Bari – mostly padres and doctors. Now nearly 200 officers in one room. A general came round.

3 October. Registering (as German POWs) in early morning. Had photos and finger-prints taken! News of 72 moving to another bungalow – all NZs, RAF, SAAF, USA officers. I swapped with MacDonald (a Yank) and went with John and Don. Did not go until aft. Plenty of room in new bungalow. Walk in aft. (Potatoes and wood) – cooked in even. and coffee. Roll call in even. Bert Steele and I lost 4 rubbers to Blackie and Andy in even, but were only 1,000 points down at end. We had v. poor cards. Went to church before we played. Heard (ie RAF bombing). 'Uncle Harold' at night (code word for RAF).

4 October. Spent most of morning in space off old bungalow in the sun. Long walk in aft. to Mühlberg. The Wachtmeister took us. Several bathed in River Elbe. John found 3 mushrooms which I cooked in even! Quite enjoyable walk. Went to bed early in even. No cigs all day!!

7 October. Walked up and down our 'area' with Blackie. Pay issued – 24 Reichmarks per officer. Nearly missed our pea-soup while collecting pay!! 6 soaps for 60 American cigs. for Don, John and I from Poles or Serbs(?). Went with Blackie. Had hair-cut (2 marks). Blackie and I had quite a long talk with Ravul Crozet in his bungalow. Heated prunes up and made an excellent (!!) custard pudding for even. meal before Don and John came back from walk. Bert and I lost by 1,400 points at bridge against Don Latham ('Bull') N.Z. and partner in evening. Very up and down. Cup of coffee in evening.

11 October. Canadian parcel issue and 25 Players. Got some pepper (ersatz), mustard (French), razor blades and small glass from canteen (2.2 marks). Sunny day after very cold night. Went to see R.C. in aft. He was dividing his bungalow's rations out. Arranged French lessons with him. Pat MacC and I played bridge with Bert and Ray Nottle in even. We were over 3,000 down; but apart from 7 hearts early on, we had very poor cards.

13 October. Showers at 10.30. Washed some clothing. Saw R.C. at 2.00. Learnt some French. Translated a bit of a newspaper. Made and cooked some (salmon) fish-cakes in evening – too wet and not enough potatoes, but very tasty!! Bert and I played Blackie and Andy bridge in even. About all-square at the end. Very even all through.

22 October. Nothing special in morn. Made some meat-roll cakes in aft. Great success! French conversation at 2.00. Got a bit of 'canary'. Bridge in even. again – MacC went 6 light on a 3-hearts call, and another time went 'spades' when he had mixed the 2 black aces up!! About 1,000 down during evening. A litre of beer in even. Olly gave me 5 cigarettes. Pamphlets dropped from air on:-
1) Air post (ie news)
2) Churchill's and Roosevelt's words.
3) Hitler's forecasts.
4) Stalin's words.

23 October. Read in morn. Short walk with Andy in aft. Bridge in even. – same game.

24 October. Communion. Geoff Dunn and I watched a practice Fr game of soccer and afterwards Fr v Holland, 2-2 when we left. Apparently we missed a free fight!! Bridge in even. (Beer in morn.) Another 'tract' – H's words.

28 October. Beer in morn. (CSM). Lecture beforehand – by a padre (Thomas) been POW in Germany for 3 years – on his experiences of different camps. French in aft. (Coffee and 'brandy-cake' with him.) Bridge – dreadful cards, lost our lead and were 3,000 down at end!!

29 October. Beer (CSM and CPL) (Fr sgt pilot). French for a bit in aft. (Had cocoa, and gave him a bit of coffee.) Bridge in even. Even worse cards than last night. Bert and Ray had an amazing run of cards. About 14,000 down at end!! (The worst 2 nights so far at bridge.) Said goodbye to Olly. Earlier I had said goodbye to Don Hutte and John Mills who left for naval camp.

30 October. The 23 officers (sick and senior) left in early morning. Gave L/Cs and P.C.s out. Drew tins out of store. News that we are not going after all (1st heard news that we were going on Wed.) Saw CSM. Arranged a walk. He came outside hut. Officer told sentry to take him off. Saw him in his quarters afterwards after he had walked back!! Watched Ping Pong instead of French. Got over 1,000 back at bridge in even. Wrote L/C home (9th).

31 October. Communion. Made porridge afterwards. Saw CSM. He did not want to come on walk again! I went with about 30 others. V. enjoyable. Went into church and climbed up to the belfry. Also had 3 glasses of beer at a pub there. V. fast pace on way back. Church in evening. Bridge in even. – a little down.

1 November. We were paid (27 mks). Wrote P.C. home (No 10). French in aft. parcel (Canadian) and 25 cigs issued. Gave prunes, raisins and a bit of bread to Russians. Read a French paper in evening.

☆　☆　☆

11 November. Armistice Day. Short parade with prayers, 2 mins silence and National Anthem at 11.00 am. French in aft. We were paid 27 marks. Spoke to Cpl Maddan (QRR) taken in Crete. Went to canteen in even. but did not drink. Spoke to Yugoslavs and 2 Frenchmen. One spoke excellent English and had a candid talk with him on the Fr. govt.

12 November. Drs Bob Burns and AN other (NZs) were supposed to have left for other camps, but there was nothing to carry their kits so they came back!! Wrote P.C. (No 12) home. Bert and I went to collect his autograph album. Chatted for some time to the Fr artist. Spoke to a French Observer in RAF. Concert in even. – in the form of a radio broadcast (not seeing the cast) – exceptionally good. Longer news incl. Hitler's speech by Hirst-Brown. Lt Col Webb spoke to us about several matters – (1) General Welcome's Fund for providing money for non-working NCOs, so we are giving a minimum of 10 marks. (2) Saluting – ORs not supposed to salute W/Os and NCOs. (3) Bob Burns left in night (ie escaped).

13 November. Stayed in bed late. Red X representative came round. News of 2 brothers at Mühlberg – one shot. Colonel put in letter of protest. French in aft. Parcel fatigue afterwards. Issued with 1 English parcel each instead of Monday, as they were wet. Rainy day. Gramophone in other bungalow in even. Not loud enough.

☆ ☆ ☆

28 November. Bob and I took a long walk round the camp. Watched volley-ball (R v Br)!! Blackie and I watched France v Holland at soccer. V. poor and v. cold. We were going to RAF v Army, but went to wrong ground. Read in even. (Got to know that we were going on Wed – on Sat 27th.)

29 November. Read in morn. Went to theatre in aft. Saw *Blythe Spirit* (Noel Coward's play) given by ORs. V. good indeed. Rather drawn-out play and poor ending. Band in attendance. Lecture on 'Life in Occupied Territories' by an RSM who was over a year in Greece. V. good talk. Clothing issue (Red X). Wrote P.C. home. Clothing parcel from home. (Clothing 1 BD trousers, 2 vests, 2 pants, 2 socks, 1 pr boots, 1 shirt, 1 boot laces.) Started cold.

30 November. Roll call as usual 7.30. Baths for our hut at 8.00. Carried kit up for disinfestation. Before we had finished the order came for our not moving after all (ie not tomorrow). Read more of book in afternoon. No French. Had a rotten cold. Crozet came to our show in evening – 'Guest Night'. Excellent show. Crozet stayed for tea and biscuits afterwards.

1 December. News that we are going on Saturday!! Took washing to be done at showers (by Russians). Finished my book. V. good indeed. French in aft. Lecture on 'Tripoli to Italy' by a Scots Guards Sergeant. Good talk.

2 December. Walked about camp with Bob in morn. French in aft. Started bridge in even, but long AR (Berlin).

Took trousers to tailors.

3 December. Issued with 1 can of Xmas parcel each. Packed again. Collected trousers from tailors. Took suitcase up to 'Search Room'. French in aft. Had tea with RC. Got a French greatcoat for the journey. Wrote L/C home (No 16). Summers had a bird (Kestrel) from England.

4 December. Roll call as usual 7.30. Handed crockery, cutlery, blankets and dixies in. Search. Down to Neuburxdorf station in a bus. Walked about down there till all had arrived. Then got into 3rd class carriages with wooden seats. Moved off about midday. V. frosty and cold day. Heating in train. Did not sleep till after midnight. Missed the 'Rapid' connection. Dresden. Bob and 'the Colonel' cheered things up by singing.

5 December. Travelling all day, but not always on the move. Had not moved much in night. Still Dresden area. Scenery dull. Bob and I played 'Battleships' and 'Hangings' for a short time!! Stomach upset with bread (untoasted). Went through no big towns. Scattering of snow on ground. Had some v. good soup and some coffee at Hirschburg at night. Woke up in night after dozing, and found the air terrifically stuffy and stiflingly hot. Opened a few windows but no difference till heating switched off from the train.

6 December. More interesting country. Arrived at Märisch Trübau.* Marched 2 kilos up to camp VIII F. Search. Issued with crockery etc, but no blankets here. We were first arrivals. Sleeping in top storey of big building – and not in little cottages as we had hoped. Central heating. 2 roll calls. Only 1 blanket for night, and I had brought that. This camp is an old boys' school. Played 'draughts' with Bob. I won all games.

7 December. Bob and I walked round outside. Got suitcase searched, and unpacked it. Put some tins in store. Was sick after pea soup. Think it must have been the bread, or possibly the journey. Went to bed. Diarrhoea. Not on roll call. Felt shivery. Could not eat anything. Took 2 laxative pills (Bert's).

8 December. Stayed in bed. A German came to see me, and gave me medicine. Nothing special. Ate a little cabbage and

---

MARISCH TRUBAU OFLAG VIII F. A large building surrounded by huts and very cold during the winter. Situated in the Sudetenland of Czechoslovakia.

potato at lunch. 'Brought it up' later (twice). Wrote to International Red X, Geneva, for mail to be sent here, and also No 17 L/C home.

☆ ☆ ☆

10 December. Our room and the next to it were fumigated, and all officers went down for a shower and disinfestation. I, being sick, moved to Blackie's room till ours was opened – and did not go down to showers (some had to go right down to town with kit, and some went in camp). I had a cold wash all over. Ate some of ration plus few biscuits, and it stayed down!! Felt well again. Finished reading book. Quite good. Started *The Unfinished Clue* by Georgette Heyer. Parcel and cigarette issue. Also pay (22 marks – 5 gone to central fund). Over 800 officers and orderlies arrived at night. Our lot showed them to their rooms. I stayed in bed, after having moved to own room. Several Modena officers came incl. Alf Evans, Glüchman, Newsome (Maj), 'Wally' Ross, Reg Sprake (was on 'report' with Boyton but turned back by Germans when 40 miles from Spanish frontier – Boyton coming here later). 2 'Aussies' Frost and Owens (who met me at Tobruk and were at Bari), and Monty Mirkin. Also Bill Bowes and F.R. Brown (Cricketers).

11 December. Got up before roll call at 11.00 (as we were v. late with 'lights-out' last night). Nothing special during day. Read. Went over to 'Mess' at 1.00. Helped Dan in even. Lights fused in our room and the next. Marked laundry. 'Brought up' my lunch.

12 December. Went to Communion – many there. Walked outside for a bit. Still very 'off my food', and brought all food up. Not feeling ill though. Read a bit. Still very cold weather. Bob and I played casino and 2-handed patience in the evening. Went to Evensong. Good attendance and band. Played 'Patience' with Lex Lamb in even.

13 December. Went on sick parade. 'Snozzle' was Dr there and gave me some pills; not to eat anything today. A full Colonel took over SBO from Lt Col Marshall. The new SBO was commander at Cos (Col Kenyon). Nothing special during day. Stayed in room. Finished *The Unfinished Clue* – quite good considering it was a detective book. The new room moved in.

14 December. Went on sick parade. Given stomach powder

and told I could eat a little today. Got some Bengers food made by Sgt Mechanen at the hospital. Ate some potatoes at lunch and also Canadian biscuit. Gave sausage away to Bob. Felt much better, but not very strong yet!! Very cold weather. Nothing to do. Had my first letter from home (Letter 4? dated Nov 18th), in which M acknowledged 2 L/C and P.C.s d October 7th.

☆　☆　☆

18 December. Made more arrangements for history lectures. Saw Radford about forming a Society. He was agreeable to taking the job on if there was a sufficient demand. He also said he would lend me his books when the educational term began. There was a meeting of all lecturers at 4.00 pm when the policy of the Educ. Offr. was given. A committee was elected – 4 offrs, incl. one representative for history and English and other minor subjects combined. I agreed to do the donkey work for history if Radford would do the rest. Played bridge in evening. We won easily. Had a cold swill in evening.

19 December. Communion after roll call. Matins at 11.00. Both services very well attended especially the latter. Very enjoyable service with good sermon. Walked round with Bert between services. V. cold day – as usual! Finished reading *Jovial Host* – quite amusing but not the sort of book I like. Radford came to see me after having contacted several officers re history etc. I am making out book registry for top 2 floors and Bungalow 8.

☆　☆　☆

22 December. Parcel issue (Xmas ones for us). 'Showers' at 10.20, the first since last camp. We put decorations up in our room (strips of coloured paper off Red X tins, and the fluffy paper (some tinsel) from parcels. Played bridge in aft. Awful cards. MacC was my partner. Beat Johnny Hall twice at chess. Debate in evening – 'That the noblest prospect a Scotchman has is the road that leads to England' (Dr Johnson). Quite amusing. Snowed at night.

23 December. Bob and Ray came a 'cropper' when sliding!!

A bit of snow-balling. Dozed a bit after lunch. Went round bungalow 12 for history books, but there were none. Johnny beat me at chess. Horse-racing' etc in evening. After winning several marks and losing it again, I came away even. (Find the lady, crown and anchor, Roulette etc.) Bob and I had tin of bacon for dinner.

24 December. Camp Ord Offr. Not much to do except making some forms out. Same in the afternoon. Beat Johnny twice at chess. Carol service in Mess at 3.30. V. good indeed (with choir). Bob and Wally Ross played Geoff Dunne and me at bridge in even. We won by 3,500 points. The bidding of the last hand went 1 Diamond, 1 Heart, 6 Hearts and we got it!! Some counterfeit chips were circulated at the 'Casino'.

25 December. XMAS DAY. Communion at 7.30. Walk with Blackie before Matins at 11.00. Both services crowded. I was Room Ord Offr – bringing up food etc. Wrote 2 P.C.s home (Nos 19 & 20). Peter Griffiths beat me at chess. Started another game. We had our Xmas dinner in even. Cotterell (N.Z. rugger player) came to it. We had beef steak and macaroni, potatoes, Canadian biscuits with raisins on, sardines on toast (savoury), plum pudding, choc biscuits and Xmas cake. Also beer and coffee. V. full!! Went to an ORs variety show. V. poor. Community singing a bit better.

26 December. BOXING DAY. Finished chess with Peter G. I won. Kicked football about in the snow. Had a cold 'wash bath' afterwards. Marked new laundry. Saw Radford about book registry etc in aft. Played bridge. Lex and I beat Bob and Crutwell (J) by 2,130 points. Beat Bob at 2-handed patience. Went to a play given by the ORs. Quite amusing.

27 December. Played Bob 2 games of patience. Lost both but won 2 in the aft. Played bridge in even. Geoff Dunne was my partner, 2,000 down. Cabaret in evening from 7-9.30. Dinner – fried Canadian meat roll, chips and pudding made of biscuits and raisins. Some went in fancy dress. All waiters (offrs) dressed up in Eastern garments. 3 issues of 'beer' and coffee. Excellent variety shows – exceptionally so when one considers the short time to prepare, lack of props etc. Roll call 10.00.

28 December. Educational Enrolment Day. I was present in dining-hall most of morning and from 3.15-4.00 in aft. I was looking after Hist, Econ, Geog and Eng. Beat Bob at patience in aft. Peter G. beat me at chess, after I had stupidly lost my queen. Bridge in even. Ray and I v. Bob and Jack C. 1,000 down. Lecture by Padre Thomas on the camps he had been in Germany; v.g.

29 December. Parcel issue (Can.). Showers. Beat Pat MacC at patience, and did not finish a game with Ray. He beat me in aft. Also I beat Bob and drew one. Bob and I played Blackie and Andy (bridge) in even. Nothing in it. Wrote P.C. home (No 21).

30 December. Broke 2 bowls in morn. Handed 2 books for Bob and me into Book Club, as can now draw one out. Dull damp day. Got the *Epic of Mount Everest.* Lecture on '12,000 miles for nothing' in aft. – describing a trip to Canada and back. V. poor. Bridge with Elton in Room 29 in even. All square. 2 letters: from M d Nov 23 and Aline.

31 December. Made a pudding with Bob in morn. Wrote P.C. home (No 22). Asked whether all kit had arrived home. Finished reading *Epic of Mount Everest.* V. interesting indeed. Watched some 'reel dancing' (mostly Scottish) after roll call in even. 'Brew-up'! Went to 'Watch Night Service' at 11.45 and saw the New Year in:

1944

1 January. Read in morn. New Year Card display in aft. Voted for best to send (a) to 'Their Majesties' and (b) the best for being reproduced to send home. I voted (a) one with 'Gentlemen . . . The King' inscribed under a batch of offr. POWs toasting the King by their beds, and (b) one of a POW looking into search-light ray and seeing his family depicted in it. Finished reading *Shackelton's Boat Journey* by Commander F.A. Worsley (re Endeavour, Elephant Isle and South Georgia etc.) V. good book. We had a New Year's Day Dinner in even. (Bully stew, Xmas pud, prunes, cake, biscuits etc.) BOW Cotterell came.

2 January. Communion after roll call. Matins at 11.00. Beat Bob at 2-handed patience! Got *What Happened in History* by Gordon Childe out of book club. Started it. Evensong at 5.30. Bridge after even roll call (8.00 pm as Cabaret finished now). Alex and I v Bert and Bob. They just won.

5 January. Very stiff after P.T. yesterday. Quite agony!! P.T. again. Parcel issue. Showers. P.C. home (No 23). Finished book. Interesting but heavy going. Blackie cut my hair in even. ARA. V. cold night. 27 degrees of frost. Rugger – England v Dominions. We won 3-0.

21 January. Got up. Feeling all right but v. 'full' in head. Ears still deaf (esp right one). Got *Clive of India* by R.J. Minney from library.

22 January. Got up after roll call. Watched skating a bit in morn. Did hist. notes (to page 320) in aft. in the newly-established quiet room (in small dining room). 20 old Italian letters received!! Went to show in even. (*London Lights and Laughter*). Quite good but not musical enough.

23 January. Communion 7.35. Matins 11.00. Hist. notes in aft. Bridge in even. Bob and I beat Maj Tilley and Johnny by 1,000.

24 January. Some of room went to bungalows in morn. Hist notes in aft. Letter d 30 Aug (Ital mail) from M (No 44). (News that 50 of my Ital letters out of 70 had reached home, and v. blacked when arrived home.) Bridge in even. Bob and I lost by 50 points to Ray N and George (Owens). V. close and interesting. Moved to Bob's old bed, and he took Crutwell's place.

25 January. Hist notes in morn. Red X letter re my change of address etc. Message form attached to send home ('Full of Confidence and mangel-wurzels!!'). Hist notes in aft. Bob and I lost by 1,300 points to Ray and George (bridge). 180 new arrivals incl C.B. (Caught in motor-boat at Venice.)

26 January. Parcel issue. Had chat with C.B. Bridge in aft. Bob and I beat Len and Bill Roach by 1,500 points. Wrote L/C No 28 home yesterday.

27 January. Baths in morn. Washed socks and 3 hankies. Did hist. notes. Made pudding with Bob. Wrote P.C. home (No 29). Bridge in even. Lost by 3,600 points – no cards at all.

28 January. Hist notes in morn. and after tea in aft. Had tea with Andy and Blackie in bungalow 30 – Andy gave me notebook and paper. C.B. brought 2 Queens Regt. to see me in even. 1 was in 1/6 in same action as I. Went to Gram. recital after even. roll call (La Boheme). Bored!

29 January. Hist. notes in morn. Gram recital at 1.30 – light music incl. Overture William Tell, Bolero and Merrie England. Hist. notes after tea. Bridge in even. Bob and I beat Bert and Mac by 2,300 points.

30 January. Communion 7.35. Matins 11.00. Was room ord. offr. Finished reading *Clive of India*. V. good. Hist. notes in aft. Bridge in even. Bob and Ray Conway beat Jimmy and me by 2,000 points.

3 February. Baths at 9.00. Hist. notes in morn. Lecture on recent agricultural history at 1.30. 1st meeting of Hist. Society in aft. Major Tatham elected President. I am Secretary!! Bob went to lecture. Brewin read paper on 'Some Observations on Causes of Modern Wars'. V. good but discussion got off the point. Radford only told me re being Sec. as I went in!! Bridge in even. Bob and I beat Jimmy and Mickey Bolton by 1,500 points.

4 February. Hist. notes in morn. Saw Maj Tatham, Radford etc. re Hist. Society. Spent long time with Radford. Few more hist. notes. Bridge in even. Bob and I v. George and Bill.

5 February. Hist. notes in morn. and aft. 2 letters from Mum (d Dec 13 and 26). News of Aline's boyfriends!! John Young! Went to theatre in even. to see *Spring Meeting*. V. good show indeed, esp Brewin as 'Baby'.

10 February. Did few notes, but reading room smokey, dusty and no fire!! V. cold day. Snowing and windy. Too cold in silence room in aft. again (fire out). Read through notes in even.

☆ ☆ ☆

22 February. Hist. notes in morn. Extra roll call in morn. Some of us in Silence Room did not hear bugle!! Lasted 4 hours till 3.00!! Read in even. Letter d Jan 18 from M.

23 February. Parcel issue. Lecture by Solomans on 'Beveridge Plan' – v. g. indeed. Hist. notes. Fixed Hist. Soc. lectures up. Started cold.

24 February. Baths. Did little notes, as feeling miserable with cold, sore throat etc. Arranged for fire in House 18 for society meeting this aft. Med. exam in morn. Hist. Society in aft. Lt Col Webb spoke on 'Growth and Development of Social Legislation in N. Zealand'. V. good. Jimmy and I played Ray and Georgie bridge in even. Draw. L/C home (30).

25 February. Gargled in morn. Had photo taken. Did hist. notes in morn. and aft. P.C. d Jan 6 from M, and L/C of 11 Jan from Aline. Gramophone in even. in room. Late for roll call as did not hear bugle!!

☆ ☆ ☆

9 March. Baths. Hist. notes. Hist Society at 5.00 pm. Padre Chutter read paper on 'Passing of Medieval Church'. Wrote L/C home (No 34). News that Peter Griffith killed while attempting to escape off train.

10 March. Identity roll call at 9.00 in gym. Hist. notes. Bridge in even.

11 March. Hist. notes most of day. Book parcel via Bari hospital (5 books) still at censor. Ray Conway and I beat Bob and Bill by 2,400 points at bridge.

12 March. Communion and Matins. Wrote L/C (No 35) home. Read in aft. Had tea with Evan Wilson (Blackie and Andy out). Went afterwards to hear orchestra in Indian dining-hall (v.g.) Bob and I beat Ray and Bill by 600 points in even.

13 March. Hist. notes. Room Ord. Offr. Bob and I beat Ray and Bill by 3,500 points at bridge in even.

14 March. Hist. notes. Went to theatre in even. J.B. Priestley's *I Have Been Here Before*. V. good. Got 4 books back from censor.

15 March. Parcel issue. Hist. notes most of day. Our room washed out. Orderlies did not come, so others carried on (I was not there). Bob and I beat Bill and Ray C by 600 points (bridge).

16 March. Baths. Hist. notes. Hist. Society in aft. Alf Adams spoke on 'Br policy in S. Africa'. Maj Tatham could not be present so I took it. Bob and I beat Bill and Georgie by 2,000 points at bridge in even.

17 March. Hist. notes most of day. Finished last four pages of *Sir Francis Drake* in even. v.g. Washed 2 prs of socks and 3 hankies. Bill went to hospital (Scabies). Radford gave me note-book.

18 March. Hist. notes most of day. Nothing else special.

19 March. Matins. Finished hist. notes on Black's *Elizabeth* in aft. Did map of Ireland in 16th century. Read in even.

20 March. Did map of Netherlands in 16th century. Did few odd notes. Read in aft. Went to little theatre in even. *(A Night at an Inn,* and *Lady from Abroad)*. 2 one-act plays.

21 March. Read most of day. 'Casino' in even. Indian fortune-teller said I would remain in Army, marry and few children, fond of travelling, brilliant career in next war etc.!!

26 March. Communion and Matins. 2 offrs went up to gate for following G. 'Snoopers' (German snoopers tried to stop us digging tunnels etc. by coming to patrol inside the camp) accompanied by procession with hunting horn and banner. Sang 'Why are we waiting' and blew horn when cart and 2 horses plus Commandant drove up road. Followed a snooper up camp road whistling 'Dead March' and sang 'Why was he born at all?'! Someone brought imitation 'movie camera' out!! Bob and I went to tea with Andy and Blackie in aft. Hist. society afterwards, when Lt Gunn read a paper on 'Historical Method'. V.g. but too involved to follow (for me anyway!!). Bridge in even. Cliff and I lost by 300 points to Bert and Bill (who arrived back from hospital today).

27 March. Hist. notes in morn. and aft. Was room orderly officer. Went to debate in 'Quest' series in even. Padre Thomas and Lt Kinlock were speakers for and against 'Does Morality indicate what God may be?' Both spoke well.

7 April. GOOD FRIDAY. Matins – went to part of 3-hour service in aft. Saw Radford re hist. society. Went to tea with Andy and Blackie in aft. and stayed all aft. Walked round before dinner. Did no history. Nothing special in even. Lost 1 game of chess to Johnny.

8 April. History notes in morn. and aft. Went to lecture by Benharem on the 'Jewish Problem'. V. good speaker in spite of bias and accent!! Bill and I beat Cliff and Lex by 4,000 points at bridge in even.

9 April. Choral communion. Matins in big dining-room (crowded). Saw Maj Tatham, Radford and Mac re history meetings. Saw Maj Finnis afterwards and fixed up for next 2 Thursdays at 3.45 in Room 55.
Wrote L/C (No 41) home, and P.C. to Mr Palmer. Watched 2 rugger matches Eng v Rest A and B. At 2nd one (4.30) I was getting ball from other side of trip wire and a 'goon' sentry

loaded etc, but was booed and laughed at by large crowd watching game and also some civilians on other side of wire!! Cliff and I lost by 2,000 points to 'Bull' and Wilf Ferry in even. Rotten cards.

10 April. Hist. notes for short time. Went to lecture by Bill Bowes on 'Cricket' in aft. Described incidents of his career with 'body-line' and 'doctoring'. V. amusing. Went to lecture by Maj Taylor in morn. on 'Sherman – the Best Modern General'. Quite good. Was room ord offr. Went to lecture in even by Padre Jackson (R.C.) in 'Quest'. 'Did Jesus Christ Rise from the Dead?' V. good but somewhat off the point at the start.

☆　☆　☆

12 April. Parcel issue. Hist. notes. Finished off craft guilds. Went to lecture on 'L.R.D.G.' V. interesting. Johnny and I lost by 2,000 points to Cliff and Bill in even. I got 6 hearts once without support from partner. I had 7 hearts to Ace, K, J and 6 Diamonds to K,J,Q. Bidding went (starting from left) 1 spade – no bid – 3 clubs – 4 hearts – 4 no-trumps – no bid – 5 diamonds – 5 hearts – 6 clubs – no bid – 6 hearts – doubled, and got it. Lovely day.

13 April. Hist. notes in morn. and early aft. Hist. Society at 3.45 – Capt Macnair gave paper on 'Duke of Cumberland'. Walked round afterwards (Note – in Hist. Soc. 'paper' was quite good, but not much in it – v. few people there – prob. due to lovely weather). Washed 4 hankies after dinner. Bob and I lost by 1,000 points to Lex and Ray C at bridge in even.

☆　☆　☆

20 April. Hist. notes in morn. and aft. Hist Soc. after tea. Capt Stuart gave paper on 'Eng – The Rise of an Industrial State'. V.g. indeed. Maj Tatham not present (rehearsing). Clothing parcel arrived in camp for me (to collect tomorrow). Wrote P.C. home (No 43). 2 roll calls and dinner not till about 3.00 pm. 6 had escaped. Finished dinner too late to play bridge (as intended) with C.B., Blackie and Andy, but went over to see Blackie. When I got there, was told that it was 5 minutes past

60

curfew time!! I went out and Evan Wilson saw me to the door but alsatian grabbed my trousers by leg after I had gone 10 yards. He growled away and also a 'goon' from along the road, so I 'dragged' back to bungalow and kicked dog away. Evan Wilson shut door, opened it, squeezed dog's nose in it, shut it, opened it, squeezed dog's nose in it, shut it, opened it, kicked dog etc. The 'goon' would not hear of my going back to main building, so I slept in bed of room next door to Blackie. The owner was in 'clink' for night for taking someone's place in roll call.

☆ ☆ ☆

23 April. Matins. New, fat Commandant Hauftman went to service and left before 'God Save the King'. Watched N. Zealand play Wales at rugger in aft. Latter won. Went to tea with Blackie and Andy. Walked round afterwards.

24 April. Saw Bill Boyton, Andy Campbell, 'Bow' and Cliff off to Repatriation Board. Went to lecture by Padre Thomas in even. on 'Revelation and Discovery'. V. good.

25 April. Cold wind. Not such nice weather as lately. No sun. Read a bit in morn. Watched Anzac parade in morn. (Anzac Day). There was an English and an Indian contingent besides N.Z.s and Aussies. After a short service they marched past SBO (Col Waddilove) and Capt Michaelthwaite (RN). In aft. watched Anzacs v. S. Africans at rugger. Latter won 17-4. Parcels (private) issued. I got mine dated 20 Jan. my first clothing parcel. It contained 1 towel, 1 toothbrush, 2 toothpastes, 6 razor blades, 1 lbs of chocolate, 1 shaving soap (missing) 1 underpants, 1 vest, 1 pr of slippers, 2 collars, 1 comb, 1 blanket, (Hx: Comforts or Longbottoms?), 1 sleeveless pullover, 1 pyjamas, 1 housewife, 1 belt, 1 tie and 1 shirt. Cleaned cupboard out. Lex Lamb got cigarettes parcel and gave us 30 each. (A few days ago, I was told that Butler's *History of England* (1815-1914) had been confiscated by censors as it 'contains several passages, openly hostile to Germany'.) News that we are going to move. No news as to where or when, but ordered to pack by tomorrow. Think we are all going to same place. Washed 4 hankies in even. and started to pack. Wrote L/C home (No 44).

26 April. Packed in the morning. Some of outside

companies started being searched. Rumours that we are going to Brunswick. Bob and I went to Blackie's room and made cocoa on fire. Walked round most of day. Nothing else special. Went to symphony concert in Indian Mess Hall in even. Too high-brow for me!!

27 April. Sunny day. Walked round with Bert most of morning. Rumours that we are changing places with a Luft Cadet Centre, that all kit and staff are going, and that first batch is to go on Saturday. (Baths in morn.) Talked to Blackie most of aft. Andy and repatriates arrived back after afternoon tea. Andy had not passed but Bow and Cliff had!! Many tales about Lamsdorff, Brit POW miners in Poland and Russians etc. Searching carried on all day. Dan and I lost by 300 points to Cliff and Bert at bridge in evening.

28 April. Nothing special in morn. Rumours that we are only going 60 miles and that last party would not go for fortnight. Searching of personal heavy kit completed. Took my suitcase to gym for search. Dance band and a few 'turns' in even. Paul Hardwicke compered. V. enjoyable.

29 April. Lex and I played Cliff and Georgie bridge. Won by over 1,000 points. In aft. I played Bert and Cliff. About even. Bob and I made cocoa in Blackie's room with Bill Seymore. 1st batch left.

30 April. Bob and I watched more companies go out, and walked round. Played Bob 'honeymoon bridge' and won by 2,000 points. Walked round with Bob most of afternoon after we had loaded truck with parcels (hot work). Cliff and Bow left with repatriation cases (from our camp). Bob and I beat Bert and Johnny by 2,000 points at bridge.

1 May. No early roll call. Stayed in bed for breakfast!! Another 3 companies left. Walked round most of afternoon. John Forsdich nearly escaped (hole and dog!). Ray and I played Lex and Johnny bridge in evening. Nothing in it. Canadian parcel issue.

2 May. Remainder plus 30 of our company left. Only the rest of our company left in camp. Walked round in morning (football field closed!). Swept room out as we have done the last few days. Johnny and Bob fixed up a 'stufa' in the room for cooking toast etc. Very successful!! I washed shirt, pants, vest, hankies and socks in warm water. Rumour that we are not, after all, going tomorrow. Collected 2 enamel wash-

62

basins from one of bungalows. Camp very quiet now. Yesterday, Gs discovered tunnel in SBO's bungalow!! Our room very quiet for last 2 days, as half have moved to a bungalow for cooking, fire etc. However, we were not cold last night in spite of having handed in palliasses covers etc. yesterday. Weather still dullish, unlike a week ago. Half Canadian parcel issue. Bert and Ray (N) beat Johnny and me by 2,000 points at bridge in evening. V. bad cards.

3 May. Swept room out. Walked round. Dozed after lunch. Walked round after tea and supper. News that moving tomorrow early. Nothing special in evening.

4 May. Roll call at 6.00 and packed afterwards. 1st party searched after roll call, and we after them. Issued with 'wurst' and marched down to station, singing last war tunes. Carried quite a lot, but managed it. Put in cattle trucks. 18 to a third of a truck. Handcuffed in spite of protests (Ray Conway!). Boots and braces taken off us. 10 guards in other side of truck. The guards were innocent-looking and mostly decrepit creatures but v. much preferable to the types who put bracelets on!! After 8 hours wait, we moved off at 4.00 pm. Many stops, but speed at times. A bucket in our part for number 1. Georgie and Wally slept in hammocks (blankets) at night, and Georgie twice fell on me. 4 slept under the seats and 12 on top. V. cramped and stuffy. All room 87 (minus Bow and Cliff) plus Hyman and 2 others in truck. Reasonable sleep. Took handcuffs off at night. We could do this by inserting penknife.

5 May. Not allowed out. Stomach ache all day. Route via Tetchen where we saw an OR Commando, Dresden, Rissa, Leipzig and Halle. Only skirted Leipzig and thus saw only a little damage. Could only see very badly out of open door on sentries' side of truck, as only ventilator on our side. Same sort of night again. Threw handcuffs out of window after dark!! The space worked out at 4 sq ft per man incl. kit.

6 May. Arrived at suburb of Brunswick* and got out when light. Our truck load was marched to the jail to be searched for throwing bracelets away. Tiring march and very thirsty, but

---

* OFLAG 79: Near Brunswick and alongside a German Luftwaffe Aerodrome – unfortunately for us! However, the two-storey buildings had basements. Food was v. scarce during the last winter of the war.

My room-mates, mostly Aussies and New Zealanders.
Standing: Ray Conway, Ray Nottle, Bill Roach, Bow
Cottrell, Jack Frost, Paul Kingsford, Cliff Nunns, Pat
McCambridge, Bernie Law, Bert Steel, Don Foote, Dan
Riddiford and Geoff Dunne.
Seated: Johnny Hall, George Owens, 'Jock' Thoms,
Wally Ross, Lex Lamb.

hot tea when got into camp. Bow and Cliff had kept corner-room for us. 20 in room fit for less than 10. Very crowded camp, and no recreational room outside. Bomb damage in sight. News that 100s of planes recently destroyed, and many killed. Aerodrome (or 2?) a few hundred yards away!! Rumour that being evacuated. News that despite precautions on journey 8 attempts to escape. Bert and I beat Cliff and Lex by 2,000 points at bridge. Put beds together in evening. Still no palliasses and v. few cupboards. Coldish night.

7 May. Wet weather. Trees further out here than Märisch Trübau. Cannot see out of camp because surrounded by fir trees. Roll calls in square. Went to Matins with Blackie in loft. Air raid alarms and Ack Ack (bombs?). Swept room and passage out before church. Mess kitchen outside wire and only providing drinks at present. (Yesterday I got 200 'Craven A' from Uncle Charlie dated 25 January.) Wrote P.C. and L/C home, the latter veiled and the former v. open eg 'I can speak the truth and even the censor cannot object to that', and then I spoke of handcuffs etc. on journey and lack of accommodation here, and finished up by saying that 'these are the facts without details'. Others wrote very piercing cards!! Lex and I lost by 1,200 points to Ray and Cliff at bridge, after playing in late aft. and evening.

8 May. Air raid in morning!! 4 waves of bombers went over to Berlin, and the last wave dropped their bombs on Brunswick. About 15 fell all round the camp, 2 of them within 1/4 mile!! Too near to be pleasant!! We think there are 2 or 3 aerodromes round us, and one is within 200 yards. Was it a reprisal to move us here? Low cloud and we could not see the planes. The evening fighters and other planes circled round below the clouds!! I did not worry till I saw stick of bombs falling on other side of damaged building opposite our room (47), and then Birnie Law and I jumped through window and down cellar!! We thought that the next would fall on the camp, as all others had fallen on the other side!! Spasmodic sun during day, but still very cold. Walked round with Bert in early aft. For rest of day, Ray (N) and I played Cliff and Bert bridge.

☆ ☆ ☆

9 May. Walked round in morning. Sunny but windy. Watched Bert's 'balancing' class in afternoon. Went to 'Music Maestro Please' in evening. Swing and tango music, and 2 excellent comperes. V. good show indeed. 2 ARA's in evening. Cig issue.

10 May. Talked to 'Irish' and Chester Williams in morn. Washed shirt, vest, pants, towel, pyjamas and 3 hankies in aft. Warm and sunny weather. ARA. Wrote L/C and P.C. home (47 and 48). Pat and I lost by 1,000 points to Bert and Cliff at bridge in evening.

11 May. Lovely warm and sunny day. Drew English parcel. Walked round etc most of day. Helped carry Canadian crates in aft. Bert and I beat Cliff and Pat by over 2,000 points in evening. Letter dated 24 March from Mum.

☆ ☆ ☆

13 May. Lovely day. Threw tenniquoits about with Thomas in morn. and aft. Sun-bathed a bit. ARA (Red). Went to Sextet in evening. Too high-brow for me!! Gs found tunnel and sentries slept in basement!!

14 May. Communion and Matins. Weather cooler in aft. Bert and I won by 1,000 points to Cliff and Pat in afternoon and evening. 5 chaps escaped in night through hole in wire (dark night).

☆ ☆ ☆

19 May. Played tenniquoits and sat in sun in morning. Lovely weather. Bombers over at lunch-time – 100s over camp. Bombers very clearly seen in flights of 18 and in perfect formation. Fighters barely visible except for very prominent 'vapour trail'. Swarms of fighters. 2 German fighters seen. A lot of tin-foil dropped in camp. Very large and extensive fires in Brunswick and pall of smoke in sky obliterated the sun. Saw 3 parachutes. Went down to Air Raid shelter once!! French POW camp set on fire (down road). Saw civilians returning from woods after 'all clear'. Tenniquoits in afternoon and then 'Scottie' and I played bridge. Won by 500 points. C.B. and I played Andy and Blackie bridge in even. V. even game.

20 May. Fine day. Had photo taken in aft. with Andy. Went to tea with C.B. and then to the Light Musical Concert in attic. Bob, John Nordee and I went to *The King's Head* in evening (a radio play in Dorothy Sayers' series). Roll call in aft. 'Attention' (G order)!

21 May. Went to Matins with Bob. Air raid during service. Ack Ack but no bombs near. Wrote L/C to Uncle Charlie and went to Evensong in aft. Bert and I beat Cliff and Pat at bridge in even. Made Red X tin withdrawals. ARA at night.

22 May. After having had toothache for last 2 days, I had the offenders out after morning roll call (Novacocaine?) Porridge for breakfast, not burnt this time (made by Bert). Air raid again at lunch-time. Heard bombs in distance and Ack Ack (usual). Very windy and cold day. Nothing special in aft. Bob and I cooked (as usual) in evening. Air attack on Brunswick between 2.25 am (tomorrow) and 3.15 am. Bob woke me up!! Dressed and went to basement because I was so cold!! Flares lit up the whole country. Heavy Ack Ack.

23 May. Cold windy day again. Bob and I cooked pancakes (yorks. pudding) for lunch. Got a greatcoat in afternoon. Bob and I cooked custard, prunes and small Red X pudding for supper. Went in to pay questions (Italy) in evening. News that offensive opened on Normandy bridgehead. ARA (yellow) at night.

☆ ☆ ☆

29 May. Room orderly offr. Porridge for breakfast. ARA from 10.30 am to 3.00 pm. Stopped playing Jock 'quoits to watch the fun!! Planes passed miles to the north. About 20 waves of 50-100 bombers counted. Several 'flights' of 12 or so passed over here on way back. Slight Ack Ack. V. warm and sunny day, and v. clear sky. Bob and I cooked eggs for lunch. Cooking interrupted by more Ack Ack. One of our 'Lightnings' came over here very low. I thought it was a Jerry plane at first, as it was so low. A lot of machine-gun fire directed at our plane, which in its turn machine-gunned the autobahn (500 yards from here). Some people saw two more 'Lightnings' at other side of camp. Had room photograph taken in morning, and Bob just missed it!! Cliff and I played Wilf Ferry and Dick Barlow bridge in evening. Nothing in it. German wireless broken down, and no communique!!

30 May. ARA during the morning. 2 'Mustangs' machine-gunned the Ack Ack near the bridge and the autobahn. Dan and I were watching from the attic windows, but a building prevented our seeing the plane (2nd one). However, we saw the Ack Ack bursts over the fields and the cattle stampeding. The plane was flying at roof-top height. Some other planes passed over, but very high. Bob and I cooked pancakes for lunch outside. 'Jock' and I played bridge in another bungalow in afternoon. We just won. Afterwards we lost 2-1 sets at tenniquoits. Bob and I went to 'Brunswick Recording' in evening. V. good dance music and variety. Started a cold. An Indian army lieutenant died of heart attack in even.

31 May. Felt miserable with cold. Sunny but strong breeze. (Yesterday I got 2 parcels of 200 Players cigs, one from

Ripponden and other not marked with sender's name. Both addressed to Oflag VIII F. A few days ago, we were told that our address was changed to Oflag 79.) ARA but no 'fun' in morning and late afternoon (both only short). Sat under trees and 'dozed most of day!! Bob got cig. parcel. News (in letter) that only next-of-kin will in future be able to write to POWs. Cooked dried apricots in aft. to go with custard made by Bob. Bob and I beat 'Jock' and Lex by nearly 5,000 points at bridge in evening. (Union Day – S.A.)

3 June. 'King's Birthday' parade in the morning. Band played: 3 cheers and National Anthem. Dressed up in BD with collar and tie for the parade!! Sunny on and off in aft. after slight rain in morn. Bob and I cooked eggs (ie powder) outside for lunch. Walked round in aft. and evening. Played bridge for short time. Cooked meat roll for dinner.

☆ ☆ ☆

6 June. Germans admit landing in France. Lost bet of German issue of sugar to Jim Alp and Cliff, as I had said it would be between 7th and 17th of June!! – one day out!! Elton had his chicken pinched by the Germans!! After long argument, he was taken to the Commandant who agreed to swap 'chick' for 2 eggs!! Rainy aft. and evening. Cooked curried salmon in evening. Cliff and I lost by 1,500 points to Bert and Ray at bridge in evening.

7 June. Wet weather. Germans made fantastic claims re second front!! Started P.T. again in aft. Felt a bit sick after it!! Cooked 'Welsh rarebit' for dinner. Bob and I played Andy and Blackie bridge in even. and won by 1,500 points.

8 June. Parcel issue. Collected contributions of cigs and biscuits for Frenchmen. Went to lecture on 'Greece' in afternoon and v.g. short history of the country. Did P.T. alone outside afterwards. Windy and cold day again. Bob and I went to *King of Sorrows* play in evening. Walked round afterwards.

9 June. Finished reading *Goodbye Mr Chips* by James Hilton, which I started reading last night. Dull and wet day. P.T. in aft. Bob and I made a cake in evening!! ARA at night.

10 June. Was Company Orderly Offr. for the day, so had to get up early. Sunny morning. Walked round a bit with Ray C. Wet afternoon. P.T. as usual. Cooked eggs for breakfast, and 'Ham' cooked bully in batter for Bob and me for lunch but it came back from mess, very 'soggy' and more like a pudding.

☆　☆　☆

15 June. Sunny and windy, with rain showers. ARA and quite heavy Ack Ack before I got up. Planes seen and bombs heard. Roll call after All Clear when I got up!! Canadian parcel issue. Spent most of day washing clothes – 7 hankies, pyjamas, shirt, vest, pants, towel and socks. Dried most of it, but rain prevented some from drying. P.T. in aft. Cliff and I beat 'Irish' (Paddy Wilson) and Wilf Ferry by 1,000 points at bridge in even. Was room ord. offr. ARA at night (asleep).

☆　☆　☆

18 June. Communion and Matins. Nothing special in aft. 'Ham' and I lost by 3,000 points to 2 KC Indian offrs in evening. A few days ago Germans announced 'secret weapon' to shell London! Bob 'took over' washing-up for a week, as I did it last week.

19 June. Warm, sunny, but windy day. Talked to the 'Balancing' Indian in morn. Sat outside in aft. P.T. 'Ham' and I played Tom Vincent (N.Z.) and Ken Hunt bridge in even. We just won. ARA at night. Germans admitted we had reached the other side of Cherbourg peninsular.

20 June. ARA just after bugle for roll call. Stayed in bed till 9.45. 3 or so lots of bombs heard. Several waves of bombers seen. I saw 2 waves. Ack Ack. Pall of smoke drifted over camp. Later on, saw 2 fires in outskirts of Brunswick from the attic. Cannot see the centre of town because of trees. Wrote P.C. (No 54) home. Warm and sunny with breeze. Later in afternoon a huge fire seen over horizon in direction of Hamburg. 'Ham' and I played Cliff and Bert bridge in even. Lost by 1,500 points. ARA at night.

21 June. Warm and sunny day with slight breeze. ARA for most of morning. Spasmodic Ack Ack and planes often heard.

My South African friends.
Standing: Evan Wilson, ? , ? , Andy Campbell.
Crouching: Paul Kingsford, 'Blackie', Chris Purdham.

Fighters seen over camp. Distributed Argentine bulk Red X food parcels in our room in morning. Sunbathed in aft. Late for P.T. so did it on my own. Did some sewing in evening.

22 June. Dull day. Walked round with Jim Alp in morn. Then read for a while in quiet room in basement. 'Ham' and I played bridge with Cliff and Ray in aft. We won. Walked round with Blackie after afternoon tea. Got 200 Players from Ripponden Comforts Fund (addressed to IV B). Blackie gave me 2 photos of the group we had taken (re Evan Wilson, Andy, Chris Purdam, Blackie, Self and two others).

23 June. Wrote L/C (No 55) home, and enclosed photo of group. Letter dated 6 April from M, P.T. in aft. Pancakes for afternoon tea (from 'mess'). 'Ham' and I played 2 Moslem VCOs (Indian) bridge in evening. Won by 2,000 points. Germans reported that 2 offrs who escaped from M. Trübau were recaptured and 'shot while attempting to escape again'. Russian offensive began!! ARA at night.

☆ ☆ ☆

70

28 June. Red X food in morning. 3 offrs. left for another camp. What for? Georgie went before Germans again for the 3-weeks'-old 'bread lorry' incident. He was told that he had to go before a court martial on 24 Aug. for 'Striking a superior' – mountains and mole-hills!! Also Paddy Webb for CM for mentioning the word 'Swines' in a letter!! Sunny and warm day. Walked round with Ray C in aft. Spoke with Blackie in aft. (Andy still in gaol!) Went to 'Bulk Issue' in evening with tango and jazz bands and a few 'turns'. Very good. Walked round with Ray C after concert till 'dog-time'. ARA at night.

29 June. 9 orderlies left for working-camp and replacements came in as only 'C' grade are allowed as orderlies in Oflags. My cold a bit better. ARA from 8.00 till 11.10. Missed the first part as I was in bed. Some people saw bomber shot down. Ack Ack much more intense than usual. Hundreds passed over camp. I saw one big formation. Many passed nearby camp. To roll call after raid and then breakfast. Washed 7 handkerchiefs and 1 pr socks in aft. Walked round with Ray C in aft. P.T. as usual. Shampooed hair afterwards. Spoke to Andy and Blackie and was late for roll call (our coy's first for counting); and got camp ord offr duty for tomorrow. Ray C again walked me off my feet in evening!! (Yellow alarm in aft.) Germans still say that the harbour of Cherbourg denied to us, as isolated strongpoints holding out.

30 June. 31 orderlies left for working-camp. I was camp ord offr!! Rainy morning. Funeral party left after roll call. Memorial service for Roy Bylmer, Wadeson and Hugh Mackenzie at 10.00. Death march, 2 psalms, hymn 'Jesus Lives', last post and Reveille. Almost faultless recording of bugle calls. Got *The Age of Catherine de Medici* by J.E. Neale out of library. Some history notes. Walked round with Ray C in evening.

1 July. 31 NCOs (supposed not to work) replaced orderlies. Sat with Andy in morning. Read in aft. Georgie and I lost by 2,000 points to Lex and Johnny at bridge in even. V. poor cards. Georgie notified by Gs that minimum sentence for conviction of his offence was 6 months' imprisonment or military detention and maximum was life impris or death!!

2 July. Communion and Matins. Spoke to OR (Cpl) from 4th Recce. I was room orderly offr. Chatted with Andy in aft. and dozed off to sleep. Did not wake for roll call and was late!!

Walked with Ray C in even.

3 July. Finished reading *The Age of Catherine de Medici* by Neale (JE). Very brief but excellent account of religious wars. Well worth re-reading at a later date. Sat outside most of day. P.T. in aft. Andy and 'Pop' (Baker?) beat a major and me by 5,000 points at bridge in evening. We had dreadful cards.

4 July. Got *Eminent Victorians (Dr Arnold; General Gordon)* by Lytton Strachey out of library. Read outside most of day. Warm and sunny. P.T. as usual. Downpour of rain at roll call, which we held in basement. Ham and I lost by 1,700 points to 2 KCOs in even.

5 July. Divided room's bulk issue in morn. (Hymn book, which arrived on Friday, still not back from censor.) Read in aft. Went to *Iolanthe* (Produced by Alan Glover) in evening. Marvellous show – the best I have seen 'in the bag'. Costumes, props, acting and music all excellent.

6 July. Warm and sunny (after dull day yesterday). Read in morning and aft. String orchestra outside from 4.00 to 5.00. Good light music. P.T. as usual. Walked round with Ray C in evening. Finished reading *Eminent Victorians* in evening. Very interesting and well written. Got my Prayer Book back from censor. Received 2 letters from home – April 16 from M and April 19 from D. from St Anne's. 3 ARAs during day, but no fun.

7 July. Lovely weather. Read outside in morn. and aft. P.T. as usual. Very poor pressure in showers (worse than usual). Went to *Libel!* in evening. Geoff Dunne in cast. Very good show – produced by Law Society. Long ARA in morn. (2 waves heard).

8 July. Wrote L/C (No 57) home. No water 'on' in aft. so did not do P.T., as could get no shower. Got a wash later. Played Jim Alp chess in aft. Drew 1-1 and I had one unfinished game in which I was a bishop 'up'. Very hot day. Got *Essay on Clive* by Lord Macaulay out of library. Went to *Iolanthe* again in evening. Wonderful show! Enjoyed it even more than last time. Terrific prolonged applause (last night of the run). Almost every song 'encored'. A 'goon' watched it. Loud singing of National Anthem. Beautiful evening. Everyone's spirits up! Had cold shower after lights out, as it was so hot. 4,000 Canadian parcels arrived in morn.

9 July. Communion and Matins. Rain in morning. Breeze

and sun in aft. Walked round with Ray C and Blackie in aft. Blackie had been in to tea. Georgie put 'Lest We Forget' in my YMCA 'Wartime Log'. Cooked meat roll for lunch. Walked round with Ray C in even. Stuck photo in 'Wartime Log'.

14 July. Read for a bit. Dull day with spell of sun in aft. Beat 'Ham' at 2-handed patience!! Walked round with Ray C in aft. Went to *The Man Who Came to Dinner* in evening. Excellent scenery and acting but the play was spoilt by crude humour (original script). Germans admitted 'fall of Pinsk and Vilna'. 1,500 Indian parcels arrived.

16 July. In the early hours of morning, woken up by heavy Ack Ack and sound of planes. Many rushed down to cellar!! I stayed in bed, half-asleep. 2 lots of Ack Ack and then 'yellow' siren went, but followed by more Ack Ack later on. Some people thought they felt distant bombing, but anyway no flares etc. over Brunswick. Went to Communion and Matins. Water left on for some unknown reason. Walked round with Ray C in aft. and then played 'Ham' 2-handed patience. Drew one all and one draw (moral victory!!). Beat Bob 2-0 in evening. Walked round with Ray C before 'Dog Time'.

17 July. Sunny after roll call but turned dull. Lex and I lost by 1,000 points to Ham and Cliff after lunch. Walked round with Bert and Ray C most of day (on and off). P.T. in aft. More Canadian parcels (2,000 arrived). ARA and planes over but no Ack Ack (asleep).

21 July. Lovely day. Sat outside in morning and read a bit. Beat Ham at patience in aft. One drawn game. Cleaned my boots!! Had a hot shower. German commandant sent 4 guards to each theatre to prevent our using them, and also stopped sending papers and German communique in to the camp, as a reprisal for our refusing to hand over a blanket each!! Letter dated 6 May. Wrote L/C (No 61) home and attached photo of room. Wrote 'Little Tommy in Deutsch-land' in my wartime log book. ARA at night, lightning.

22 July. Heavy rain in morning. Roll call in the basement. Dull during rest of day. Nothing special. Beat Bob at patience and drew 2-2 with 'Ham'. 2 ARAs during day but no 'fun'. German ban still on news, papers and theatre. 2 guards at the theatres. Went to lecture on 'The Court of Criminal Appeal' with reference to the case of Adolf Beck. Very interesting. Went for over the usual hours fast walking with Ray C in evening.

23 July. Went to Communion. Horses and carts came on roll call together with 90 guards and about 30 or 40 other 'Goons'. Hid 2 private and one G blanket in my case and left one on my bed!! 'German parade' (!!) but eventually we fell in for roll call. All guards lined up between us and House 8. Not allowed in after 'dismiss'. The Germans searched Houses 2L and VIII and took all German blankets. We had to keep 5 metres from the guards. Incident with G captain at other end, and guards advanced at 'on guard' position!! One of our colonels got a jab!! One G L/Sergeant and one *ober-gefreiter* were objectionable. We had to remain beyond the road. Padre Chutter put notice up about postponement of church services, and goons called interpreter for explanation!! Could not go into bungalow till after 11.00. Germans got all but 500 of required blankets from the two houses, and got remainder from House 6. We had previously refused to be left with only one blanket, as the MO said two was minimum for health of camp and especially those suffering from malaria. Late breakfast and then lunch. Sunny but windy day. Talked with Andy in aft. Church at 5.00. During the service I had noticed someone behind Ray C and me singing in a loud and hysterical voice. It got worse in last hymn culminating in National Anthem, when even the choir looked over our way. Just before and during the 'blessing' he collapsed on his stool, his glasses fell off, and he sobbed out loud. Two church-wardens picked him up and took him to hospital. On the way out he shouted in a hysterical voice that he was all right, leave me alone; it's lovely; I'm sorry etc. and finally shouted 'Merry Xmas'!!! Apparently he often had fits and thought he was Mohammed and also sunbathed in the rain!! Walked round with Ray C and then Trevor Atchley in evening. Had very interesting talk with Trevor on subjects such as the international situation, Jews, the Irish, RCs, post-war Empire and the Monarchy. German ban on news, theatre and papers until tonight, ie 3 day's corporate punishment. (Geneva Convention?!)

24 July. 20 July Bomb Plot! All the Germans giving the Nazi salute, instead of army one. Papers etc. into camp. Walked round with Ray C in aft. Went to the theatre with Bert in evening. Queued for the extra seats. It was a revue of all popular dance tunes from 1914-43; entitled *Shall We Dance?* V. enjoyable, but it was not up to expectations – due to first night? ARA, AA and planes at night.

25 July. Dull day, nothing special. Beat 'Ham' at patience. German Commandant found tunnel near future main entrance!! Walked round with Bert in evening. (Lecture on 'Divorce' in aft.) ARA at night.

3 August. Lovely day. Eng. and Can. parcel issue. Did a few more 'War Notes' for Johnny. P.T. in aft. Walked round in aft. Curfew at 9.00 pm (because of move tomorrow?).

4 August. Reveille at 6.00, but did not get up till later on, when Ray C made a 'brew'. About half the companies moved into new compound. Our hosts 'organized' the move. All cupboards had to be emptied and beds cleared of all except palliasses, and these were then carried through to new compound with stools. Searched on way through. All companies had to pack kit, and march outside the camp and in other entrance to be searched by security police (similar to Gestapo). They were 3 hours behind time at one stage, but the searchers soon caught up and passed the rest through quickly. We helped carry tables etc. outside the gate. To crown all, it poured with rain in afternoon and everyone's palliasses were soaked. We moved into our new room (3E) after afternoon tea. Bob, Jock and I left other room and were joined by Wilf Ferry, 'Kloppie' Paddy Wilson, John Williams, Tony Jacobs, Duncan Gray, Jim Alp, Gordon Clifton and Roy Pellant. Cleaned room out and got settled in. Jock and I beat two others by 1,800 points at bridge in evening. I missed calling 7 Hearts!!

5 August. Coffee at 6.00 am. Very cold at that hour so I got back to bed for a bit!! Moved off with light kit and food at 7.00. Searched by security police (civilians). The one who searched me succeeded in upsetting my sugar!! There were well over a dozen searchers. After we had passed through, they searched all our kit and the buildings of the 'old camp'. Spent early morning looking round the area. The garages at end of camp were completely demolished except for one partition, the house next to it was about as bad, and the one inside camp area had burst outside and penetrated the cellar. In the latter, there was a blood stain on the wall, and Andy says that there was another inside shelter! Spent some time with Andy who was drying his palliasse!! Lovely day. We left our kit in the attic of house near other entrance. Air Raid in morning!! Watched formations of and single aircraft for some time. Distant rumbles (Brunswick). Raid started in earnest about 1.30. Shrapnel rained down and bombs on this side of Brunswick. Saw target markers and also 2 planes on fire (one in left engine and one in tail) – but believe these were all right. Some saw one plane catch fire and break in two, but only one parachute seen. Hundreds and hundreds of bombers over. I went to shelter when I saw 2 target indicators and formations of planes immediately to the north and coming towards us!! I got down in time and the ground rocked like a boat! Stayed for just over five minutes by when they had passed over!! These bombs fell on aerodrome, and 2 sticks fell this side of railway in the fields. The group of houses a 1/4 of a mile off were badly damaged. One bomb (the nearest) fell 100 yards from new main entrance!! Windows blown in House 2L. Palls of smoke practically all round camp especially from aerodrome, direction of bombed houses, and Brunswick town. 'Goons' all went on rescue and demolition work – they had to saw door to get a demolition cart out of building of which the key was lost!! The whole camp was not opened up till 6.00 pm. Water and electricity off, the former not properly on for rest of day. Long (3/4 hour) roll call in evening. Made 'recce' of attic in evening to see bomb damage. Some plaster had been shaken down from ceiling of our new room.

6 August. Received 150 Rothmans, as my name had been provided by Uncle Algy. ARA all morning. Saw 5 vapour trails pass over the camp, and later watched a 'dog-fight' from attic of bungalow 7 in a northerly direction. The vapour trails after circling round and round were diving in and out at each other. Saw burnt-out factory about 1/4 mile away (from yesterday's raid). Was speaking to Radford when an odd Ack Ack burst went up, and he immediately shot off for the shelter!! (Some people are jittery!) Lovely day. Water off during most of afternoon. Did a lot more 'War Notes' for Johnny during afternoon and evening. Made tin withdrawals list out. 2 distant sirens at night, later followed by local 'all clear'.

7 August. Hot and sunny day. Chatted with C.B. and Blackie in morning. Jack Te Puni said the near bombs were dropped by a plane which was hit. Wrote P.C. (No 65) home. Rumours that accumulation of mail and parcels had received direct hit at the station in the last raid. Started reading *Gone With the Wind* by Margaret Mitchell. Did more 'War Notes'. Walked round with Ray C for over an hour in evening. Water off most of day. (Repairs?)

☆ ☆ ☆

10 August. Helped Blackie move books etc. to new library in house 2L in morning. Did more of Johnny's notes in afternoon – good revision for me. Practically impossible to do any serious reading with things so unsettled as they are now. Dull day with slight rain in morning, but warm. Jock and I beat John Luntz and John Williams by 2,000 points at bridge in evening. Planes over at night. 2 heavy lots of Ack Ack when planes (single?) came over the camp. Loud whining noise after second barrage when shrapnel was falling like hail. Bombing in the distance. Bob saw coloured tracer shells going up after 'all clear'!! (Parcel issue in morning.)

11 August. Watched French 'commando' moving new kitchen stove into camp. Sunny and warm, but cloudy and a breeze. Read in morning. Went to the first in a series of discussions on the Archbishop's (of Canterbury) book *Christianity and the Social Order*. Padre Rogers spoke on the first 3 chapters of the book (brief history etc. of why the church must intervene and concern itself with social affairs etc.) Jock and I had our hair cut by Blackie. Did more of Johnny's notes in evening (up to 1763).

12 August. Sunny and warm, but windy. Read outside in

morning and early aft. Walked round after tea. Read *Upstage* and spoke to Andy. P.T. and shower. Went to Eugene O'Neill's *Ah, Wilderness* in evening. V. good acting and excellent 'props' but much too drawn-out – lasting almost 3 hours. Air Raid soon after 'lights-out'. Rumbles in distance and then Ack Ack. Then we heard the 'Express Train' noise, so discretion being the better part of valour, we went down to the shelter!! Raid lasted half an hour on Brunswick. Saw flares before going to ground. Huge glow over Brunswick after the raid. Many fires at other side of town. Jim Alp and I went up to attic after bombing over, but not much to see. Very dark night, and difficult to find one's way about. Electricity (incl. boundary lights) off all night and until tomorrow afternoon. We thought we heard more bombing to the north.

13 August. Did not wake up for early service. Went to

Another room group.
Standing: H.C. Klopper, Roy Pellant, Tony Jacobs,
Bob Melvill, Wilf Ferry.
Seated: Gordon Clifton, John Williams, Paul Kingsford,
Paddy Wilson.

Matins. V. good sermon by Rogers on 'Love your Enemies'. Read in afternoon. Had room photo taken. Walked round with Ray C in evening. Water off most of day (as usual now!). Distant Ack Ack (and bombing?) at night.

14 August. Fine, but very cold north wind. Read most of day. Jock and I beat Andy and Blackie by 2,400 points in evening. ARA – distant Ack Ack (and bombs?).

16 August. ARA all morning and 3 or 4 waves of bombers passed over to the north-eastwards, and later returned far to the west. One of our fighters also seen – on its own. We should have drawn parcels, but the 'goons' were away to meet the new arrivals (who did not come!!). Sunny and warm day. Wrote 2 P.C.s home (Nos 66 and 67). Read in aft. Jock and I beat Sisterton and Mike by 2,800 points at bridge in evening, after we had lost 1,200 points in the last hurried rubber. Usual ARA and Ack Ack in evening. Letter d 20 May from home.

18 August. Warm and sunny day. Read in morning. New arrivals arrived at lunch-time. Looked very smart and fit and recently captured in first few days of Normandy landing. Went to German 'talkie' called *Atlantic Hotel* in evening, but came out after two reels. ARA and Ack Ack as usual in evening.

19 August. Read in morning and early afternoon. Lovely day (warm). Talked to Blackie before roll call. Went to see *London Pride* a musical revue in evening. Poor show on the whole, and it did not go with a swing. Curtain down while band played between scenes. The second half was much better, and included a scene from *Perseverance* and very good 'props' effort of neon-lights in Piccadilly Circus. No ARA at night!!

20 August. Went to Communion and Matins. Lovely hot day. Read outside in aft. Walked round with Ray Conway in evening. No ARA again!

21 August. Lovely day again. Finished reading *Gone With the Wind* – excellent book – about the best I have read. Letter-card dated 25 July (Air Mail again) from Mummy. Moslem feast of

Ramadan started – constant wailing from House 2L!! Wrote L/C (No 68) home.

22 August. Lovely day. Beat Jim at chess. Went to library and got *Marlborough* by Sir John Fortescue and *A Short History of the English People* by L.R. Green. Read a bit in aft., and then waited a long time for water to come on – eventually had to go to basement for 'shower'. Received 2 letters: from Mummy dated 30 April (and 2 photos), and Margie dated 26 April (and 2 polyfotos). Chatted with Blackie. Germans admitted allied columns south of Paris. Went to *Sweeney Todd* (The Demon Barber of Fleet Street) in evening. Amusing show. Water off till late at night, and everyone waiting to get some to drink!! Hopeless water supply since big raid on Brunswick. Rumour (from Snooper) that raid planned by Czech partisans for 20th of month that we left Trübau.

23 August. Parcel issue. Lovely day. Read most of day. Walked round with Ray C in evening.

24 August. Lovely weather until smoke obliterated the sun!! Air Raid. Saw 2 waves pass over in the distance (to the east). Later on, waves of bombers approached camp, and I saw the bombs and silver paper released just over the camp (Niemo factory). Went down to shelter of house 7. 'Hell let loose' between 11.45 and 12.15 and the shelter rocked. Eventually we went on top to see a picture of devastation. Trees ripped to pieces and cut in half; and everything was riddled with shrapnel. Hundreds of anti-personnel and incendiary bombs had fallen inside the camp, and the sides of every building were riddled with shrapnel from A/P bombs. Every building had holes in roof where A/P bombs had dropped, but they had not penetrated the concrete floor. Our ARP Wardens had done a great job putting out incendiaries and marking off unexploded incendiary and A/P bombs. The German officers' mess was on fire after receiving a direct hit from one of the 1600-lb bombs dropped. It burnt out almost completely, but our own cookhouse at the end was intact except for the roof and first floor. 2 more bombs fell at main entrance near house 2L; and the craters were over 12 ft deep. 3 more bombs fell inside the 'wood' (in the camp) and made similar craters – Bill Roach was in a hole near these bombs, but got off with slight head wounds. One bomb fell next to OR's building, and made the building untenable for living in;

so ORs moved into house 2L. 2 or 3 big pines were completely uprooted. Both of ruined buildings at south end received hits, and were set on fire. Wire blown down in several places. The garage just outside the concrete (near wire) at SE end was destroyed by fire. A horse was killed by blast on the concrete. A bird was also flattened against the ground! Everywhere outside was hit with something, and a pall of smoke and dust surrounded the camp. The aerodrome and the factory seem to have been the main objectives. The railway was also hit. Colonel Kilkelly and an Indian Subadar major were killed, and 9 others including Maj Newman and Butler-Shaw were badly wounded (6 slightly). The nice old German Hauptmann who counts us was killed, and also the regular Sgt-major chap who supervised working parties inside the camp. Also about a dozen other guards were killed. All windows in the camp were shattered. Cleaned up inside after the raid. The pine forest was burning in parts. The water and electricity were both off. Helped move food from cookhouse to basement of 2L. German fire-fighters arrived later on. Variety show with Tommy Sampson's band outside in evening. The 'Nutmeg Grater' provided free tea in afternoon and coffee in evening. We made some coffee with 'pond-water' out of leaks on hosepipes, but it tasted horrible in spite of sterilization and anti-taste tablets!! Some 8 wounded were taken out of hospital in evening. Pea soup from the cookhouse in evening. SBO's roll call at 4.00 to see if anyone missing. SBO is now Capt Michaelthwaite RN since Colonel Waddilove, Lt Col Stirling and 2 others left for a straflager a few days ago. During today's raid, the commandant was away at the court martial. Georgie Owens got 2 weeks' solitary and Paddy Webb got 2 months (for calling Commandant a 'swine' in his letter). 2 others also received sentences. Paddy Webb says it was a fair trial, and the defending officer (a German) was very good. They saw much damage on way up, but civilian population were quite friendly although homeless. No lights in evening. Goons putting fires out at night.

25 August. No breakfast or lunch provided from mess, as we were not allowed into the cookhouse. Helped clear up the rubble (slates etc., which we tipped into bomb craters. We could see no noticeable damage outside camp area; but the factory and aerodrome are hidden and they both caught a 'packet'. Looked for and then collected water from far bungalows. Water later came on in our house, and I had a very welcome wash in basement. Water soon went off again. Cold meals, still no electricity. Rescue squad still busy in cookhouse block; and a few bodies extricated. ARA (yellow) in morning, and great relief when 'all-clear' went!! Details of yesterday's raid sent to Red X and 'Protecting Power' (ie Switzerland) by SBO. Filled diary in during afternoon. Wrote P.C. home (No 69). Peter's birthday. The assistant commandant was in the camp hospital yesterday immediately after the raid to see our wounded, and then asked for a doctor to go out to wounded Germans. We had been using the outside latrines since yesterday's raid (even at night). Big queues there today (!!) but more going to be dug. A German General came round yesterday. Heard that an officer called Knight had died after leaving for hospital yesterday. Major Radcliffe was commended by the SBO for carrying A/P bombs away and taking the fuse out. SBO also thanked fire-watchers etc. Cooking and brewing-up done individually. Another of yesterday's big bombs fell between House 1 and German OBs quarters, and many more fell outside the wire at the s.w. corner of the camp. Claude Godwin and tango orchestra played light music on concrete in evening. 192 new arrivals came from Moosburg late in evening. They had been in Leipzig when it was bombed. Mostly old Italian captures. ARA and AA late at night. Spent 3/4 hour in shelter – all our room went down!!

26 August. Finished reading *Marlborough* – especially interesting passage on old type of warfare. V. hot and sunny day. Still no electricity, but water on first thing in morning. Still no cookhouse, and spent most time brewing up and cooking. ARA in morning, but shelter not necessary this time!! Goons still working on debris, craters and damaged wire. Yesterday afternoon we paraded when the hearse left the camp. The Indians had a service in morning. Drains blocked up in the camp except for houses 1 and 2 – desert (roses) 'beehives' and swill sumps being dug. Had a shower in house two. We sent a wreath to the deceased Germans. Peter Brewin's sextet and choir in evening – extracts from *Tom Jones* and *The Pirates of Penzance*. AR at night.

30 August. Dull and cool day. Parcel issue. Read on and off. Helped carry pine tree to Coy cookhouse and later chopped up wood (blisters!!). ARA in afternoon. Still no electricity or drainage. Heard that 10 goons in clink for not putting fires out!! Rained at roll call. Walked round with Ray C in evening. ARA yellow at night. Letters from Mum dated 8 May and Margie d 29 May.

31 August. Very wet day. Went to see Tuckwell and Jones Stamp and stayed for some time. Heard that André Kempster got a posthumous GC for smothering a grenade with his body after twice dropping it; he lost a leg and an arm before he died. Maj Tissington of 1/7th received a battalion, and Bishop was 'purged'! 'Reggie' Grieve of 8th (145) was wounded. Maj Evertt made CO of 9th. Tim Till went to staff college. Kempster had married 'someone else'. Tuckwell had not married Margaret Bray (who got a post as matron in North Wales), but Tony Peel was 'Best Man' at Tuckwell's wedding. Hugh Beesley had been killed (at sea?) and both daughters married. Armitage was some time ago made 'Ack and Quack'. Lord Savill had gone to India. MacClean had been made a Home Guard adjutant (?). Holroyd was still with 145. Tony was hurt when playing against Newton-Thompson etc. Talked to Evan Wilson in aft. An Indian VCO (a ghat) was shot by a sentry when he was reaching for a tenniquoit – although he was this side of trip-wire. Sentry obviously out to shoot someone as he had pointed rifle at someone else earlier on, and it was too much of a good shot (through head) to be unpremeditated. The sentry was booed on way to guard-room, and later on was seen under arrest. Spoke to 'Ham' in even. 'Yellow' warning at night. Wrote 2 P.C.s home (Nos 70 & 71).

1 September. Sunny at times, but cold and windy. Brewed up coffee with Blackie in morning. Read on and off during day. Shower in aft. 'Kloppy', Probin and another left for hospital in morning. Jim Alp had caterpillar in aft!! I forgot to mention before that the corresponding building to the Orderly Room but outside the wire was also destroyed by fire in recent raid. Went to 'Target for Tomorrow' display in aft. – which set forth various town-plans of the past, and suggested improvements in lay-out, housing, recreation, factory buildings, roads, etc. Figures given in Bournville pamphlet said that private gardens on their estate added 2/– on average to each household's budget per week (£58/15/– per acre per year), which is 6 times the average yield per acre of land under cultivation – while 25 people live in the acre of former. 'Red' warning before I got into bed, and 'yellow' later on for a long period – one of our planes flew low over aerodrome, and light and heavy Ack Ack opened up – went to shelter for few minutes.

2 September. Sunny morning, but drizzle in afternoon. Read a bit. German papers admitted fall of Amiens and Verdun. Went to Art Exhibition – very good, especially some paintings of recent raid. News that repatriees going soon – however, we shall all be off in a few weeks!! Germans admitted fighting in Arras area. Went to 'Night Light' in evening – a programme of news from home, a short radio-play and musical items – surprisingly good show.

☆ ☆ ☆

4 September. Said 'goodbye' to Cliff Nunns, Bow Cotterell, Bill Boyton and Mick Nugent in evening, as they were standing by for repatriation.

5 September. Sunny at times but windy. The 'repats' went off in the morning. Germans putting electric wires up in camp – some of houses came on for few minutes before boundary lights, but then went off again until 10.00 pm. Read a bit. Went to Claude Godwin's Tango orchestra at Nutmeg Grater – very good, despite playing in the dark to start with. Woke up late at night to Ack Ack and planes. I went down to shelter for some time.

6 September. Sunny but windy day. Helped Blackie make out a nominal role in morning. Germans admitted fall of Dieppe etc, Antwerp, Brussels, Louvain, Vaux, N. of Nancy, and Dijon – also that whole of s. western France evacuated. Germans extended lights to houses 2L and 8, so only 1 and 2 are now without them. Helped to dig more of pit where sewage is blocked in aft. Went to lecture on Preparation for Invasion, and FFI in aft. – very good. Finished reading *Trafalgar* – good account of condition of Navies. Spotted with rain in evening, but Claude Godwin played at Nutmeg Grater – enjoyed it very much as usual. Lights 'on' in evening. Forgot to mention that several buildings in SW corner of wire (outside) had been destroyed in last fortnight's raid. ARA 'Red' before 'Lights out'. Parcel issue.

7 September. Sunny and warm in morning, but windy and cold after lunch. Washed pair of socks and 8 handkerchiefs in morning. Cleaned my boots – optimistic!! Boots went in for repair. Got *History of English People* from Educational library. Had four letters in afternoon – June 9 and July 1 from Mum. Yesterday we received advice from Red X to go on to ' parcel' owing to the war situation (supplied to Switzerland). Went to John Ditchburn's Dance Band at Nutmeg Grater in evening – too windy and cold to enjoy it; also the music kept blowing about!!

9 September. Sunny at times, but windy and cold. Read most of day. AR on Brunswick at night. The blast of land-mines found its way to the shelters over half a dozen times – thought it was blast from heavy AA guns, but heard afterwards that it was not. Nearest bomb was in Canal zone about ½ to 1 mile away. A large fire in Brunswick and also one to the SSE (someone said also nine to the north west). One of our windows (near my bed) was blown in, and plaster fell from ceiling. A door was blown in in House 2. Several windows and tiles blown by the blast – must have been very heavy bombs. Birnie Law and others thought a plane came down to the west.

12 September. ARA from 10.30 to lunch-time. Waves of planes passed over to the NNE distance. Later on, waves passed westwards to the north, and AA opened up on a few planes (fighters) above the camp. Went to shelter for a bit. Others saw the formation to the north drop 4 or 6 markers to the NNE (Hanover direction) and then change direction. After a very cold night (as usual these days) the sun was very hot in morning and early afternoon, but the wind got up at tea-time. Went through fractions and decimals with Paddy after lunch. Read during rest of day. ARA 'yellow' before roll call – single plane and AA over. ARA at 10.20. Went to shelter but nothing happened. Went to shelter again after 'yellow' when planes and AA overhead. Back to bed after 12.00. Scores of rifle shots heard from Brunswick direction.

16 September. Dull day with sun at times. Short 'yellow' alarm in morning. Read most of day. Went to tea-time music at the 'Rum Pot' (ex-Nutmeg Grater), but an ARA cut it short. Paddy and I went to 'Rum Pot' in evening (8.00-9.45) Tommy Sampson's band for first and last half hour with 3/4 hour cabaret in between. Latter was excellent with Tom Meehan as compere and Bill Hollingshead's orchestra of 22 pieces. Very good laughter and the whole thing went with a swing. There was a 'bar' for snacks and drinks – for 'bully marks', and tables in front which are booked for meals before the 'show' (50 and 35 'bully marks' for a dinner)!! Short ARA before midnight. Went to shelter. Woke up later on (3.30 circa) to find boundary lights on, flares over Brunswick and AA – all while a 'yellow' was on!! Went to shelter. Blast felt by some. Most bombs fell on other side of Brunswick, and nearest was at least ½ mile. The eastward roofs of houses 7 and 6 were bashed in in 4 places – doubt as to whether AA shell casing, or whether an AA shell burst near perimeter wire or bomb on aerodrome? I heard the bang.

18 September. 'Yellow' alarm in morning. Dan said that roofs damaged in Saturday's night raid were due to blast from a bomb on the aerodrome. Still cannot use drains in our house (since 24 Aug). Had shower in house 5 after roll call and before 'breakfast'. Read in morning and early afternoon. Went to pictures of 'Shorts' in aft., but electricity failed. Went again in evening – all silent including Olympia 1936, a Charlie Chaplin etc. Germans admitted landings in Holland yesterday – airborne. Received L/Cs from Aline dated 21 July and Mum dated 10 Aug. – 2 lines of Aline's censored (re Newbury). Wrote P.C. home (No 76). Funds for Red X Week amounted to 200,000 Reichmarks – poor response, as only just over half way to our aim of £24,000. Lights went out at 9.30 and ARA at 10.00 – all clear, lights on, lights off, a flash, a bang, shelter for the second time, all clear, yellow!! – all in a short time. Went to bed after last yellow (12.00). AA and planes over. We could not understand the flash and bang – too brilliant for AA. Some thought it a (photographic) flare and a bomb, but (G)QM said a plane crashed (G?).

19 September. I was room 'stooge'. Peeled spuds in morning. Beer issue, as we have often had lately. Dull weather. ARA in morning, and 'yellow' in aft. – distant rumbles before the latter. Walked round with Blackie after roll call. I had won a prize from lottery of dead Indian's kit (the one shot) to go to his next-of-kin – my prize was mostly underclothes which I did not want. Went to choral society in evening. After an introduction of songs, the choir of 40 sang Tennyson's 'The Revenge'. V. good show indeed. Beat Roy at 2-handed patience in evening. No ARA at night!

25 September. More 'browned off' than I have been for months!! – due to (i) drizzly and cold weather, (ii) food and cigs scarce, and (iii) unsettling news!! (Arnhem). Also started a cold. Read most of day. Spent some of aft. in library. Got *Memoirs of Colonel Hutchinson* by Lucy Hutchinson (Crom-wellian period) out of library. Letter-card dated 13 June from Mum: – Understands 'special type' of gramophone records; 'simply marvellous' film on POWs; 'Uncle Harold goes up to London each day!' (Mum understood my coded message re air raids on Brunswick camp and reported our position to RAF.) The Germans posted a notice on cookhouse wall, saying that escaping is 'no longer a sport!', that they had captured a secret pamphlet on 'irregular war' and 'gangster' methods, that we had used terrorists, bandits etc., and that they had created 'death zones' all over Germany where anyone would be shot – to safeguard their industry, 'provisional front', L of C etc!! It said that escaped POWs lives would not be worth anything at all!! (The notice had been

87

pulled down by tomorrow morning!) Lights went out at 9.20.
– yellow, I suppose.

☆　☆　☆

28 September. My cold much better. Cloudy but sunny day
till late aft. ARA at midday for nearly 2 hours. Spent most of
time in shelter. Many formations of bombers and fighters
were seen all round camp, but local Ack Ack did not open up.
Turning markers dropped over Brunswick. One fighter
(British) machine-gunned aerodrome from low altitude. Read
in aft. Walked round with Jim Alp in morning. Went to cinema
in evening – a German silent film called *Romance* (musical) and
German news reel of Cassino, Nettuno etc. Both quite good.
ARA before 9.30. Went to shelter. Also again at 3.30 am. Went
to shelter. Local AA and flares to the west and SW in first raid –
bombing in distance (Brunswick)!!

☆　☆　☆

30 September. Dull and cold day. Was room ord offr. ARA for
1 hours after lunch. Went to shelter. Lots of planes all over,
but clouds hid them. AA (incl. local). Distant bombing to the
west (NW and SW). Went to tea-time music (Peter Silvester),
but it was lifeless so I did not stay. Read a bit. Lights off but no
ARA at night. One 'scare' when red flare appeared over
'drome (no planes!!).

1 October. Went to Communion and Matins. Damp and
rainy day. My cold broke out again – in other nostril!! Read.
Put clocks back one hour at night. Marked laundry. ARA at
1.00 am. Went to shelter. Flares and local AA some bombs
quite close, and bombing quite heavy. Birnie Law watched
from attic and said camp clearly marked out by flares (?), and
he said aerodrome bombed. I don't think it was as near as
that, but think that Braunschweig and somewhere NNW were
bombed.

☆　☆　☆

3 October. Sunny morning, but turned dull. Walked round in
morning. Noticed a damaged village to the right of the near

white bridge and to the left of where last night's fire was. Germans issued mail out at 10.00 am. Long queue, so I did not get mine until 11.30. Letters dated Sept 9th and 5th from Mum and Aline. (Mum wrote from Scarborough and said I ought to be home before I got the letter!! Aline again wished me many happy returns of Sept 22nd!! She and Peter had seen Vernon Watson in Bradford, and were introduced to Albert Wheelan and Charlie Kunz!!) Wrote L/C (No 80) home. 2 or 3 returned from Stalag XIB (?) yesterday having been for dental (or eye?) treatment. They met some of Arnhem POWs, who were mostly burnt from flame-throwers or who had bullets still in them, and some had gangrene due to delayed medical attention. The new prisoners gave the war another month – an optimistic opinion for new 'kriegies'. Issue of German 'tea' – many people now smoking it, and some have tried 'dried cabbage'!! Bob and I played Wilf and Paddy bridge in evening – nothing in it when ARA stopped play. 2 unaccountable bangs after 'all clear', and my bed-boards collapsed (possibly because we chipped them to get fuel for brew-ups) when I sat up!!

6 October. Turned out sunny in the end. 136 new arrivals in the camp (from Arnhem). Bert Ash came in our room. Long ARA in morning. (Capt Michaelthwaite (RN) left for Senior Officers camp. Col Brown (IA) took over SBO. In ARA, a few planes seen and also vapour trails to the NE. Nothing special in aft. Lights off most of evening. 3/4 hour ARA. Went to shelter. Bombing (?) to the NW.

7 October. Lovely day. Clear sky and quite warm. ARA from 11.00 till 2.00. Terrific roar of planes to the south. Saw AA. Bombing in area somewhere south of Brunswick. Could not see planes – v. high, so went to shelter. Some fighters (?) came overhead. Had cold shower in aft. Went to cinema to see German film but, after a late start due to our hosts having broken the film, the electricity went off after a few minutes. Went on to Rum Pot afterwards. 3 bands played – 'Pitso' and small string orchestra (v. poor), the 'Ginger Snaps' (v. good), and Tommy Sampson with 4 saxophones, 1 trombone, 3 trumpets and himself, drummer, pianist and guitarist.

Tommy played his 'best yet'. Thoroughly enjoyed it. Mostly old pre-war popular tunes, and v. well put over (3 or 4 at a time). Lights off most of evening, but no ARA.

☆ ☆ ☆

12 October. ARA in morning. Roar of planes sent us to shelter for a bit. Could not see planes, as cloudy sky. Cleared up later on, and sun came out in aft. Got *Scenes et Tableaux de la Restauration* by R. Mabille de Ponchiville out of library. Read in sun before aft. tea. Jim and I went to cinema again! – the 'goon' late in turning up, and then the sound-track broke down!! After a disjointed first reel, it was discontinued! Went to Rum Pot at 5.00 pm – quite good Gilbert and Sullivan programme – mostly solos. ARA in evening. Went to shelter for a while.

☆ ☆ ☆

14 October. Washed 6 hankies and 2 pairs of socks in morning. Finished reading *Memoirs of Col Hutchinson* in aft. Walked round with Jim in aft. and read a bit of French book. Jock and I beat Roy and George Marrs by 1,800 points at bridge in evening. 'Yellow' alarm after 'lights out'. 'Red' alarm from 2.00 am till 4.00. Huge fires over Brunswick and pall of smoke over the camp. Felt a lot of blast in shelter. (Did not go down till flares dropped.) Very heavy raid indeed, but fires on other side of town. The nearest incendiaries were supposed to have been 1/3 to 1 mile away.

15 October. Did not wake up in time for Communion, after last night. Huge fires still raging in Brunswick – even bigger than ever. Smoke obliterated the sun in the morning. Must be oil or rubber burning; and smoke stretches high into sky and then fades into the eastern horizon. ARA after breakfast – heavy bombing to the NW. 3 vapour trails (recce?) seen over Brunswick, and another later on after all clear. Collected 200 Players from Ripponden Comforts Fund. Cannot get next-of-kin till tomorrow. Went to United Services service at 11.00 am – Padres Hamilton (Presbyr) and Rogers took the service. V. good sermon by latter. Lovely day in afternoon. Read in aft. Lights off most of evening. ARA – AA and bombing (?) to the

NW. Went to shelter for a bit. Fires still burning in Brunswick at night. My shirt missing (tomorrow) as laundry was bombed. GW and UAF (Guided Weapons and underground armament factory).

☆ ☆ ☆

17 October. The other laundry was also supposed to be bombed, so I have also lost my vest. This week's laundry (due yesterday) was returned to me unwashed. ORs went to town yesterday. Main bakery destroyed. ½ Can. parcel issue. Made withdrawals list out, as OKW order now disallows food inside the camp – so we have to take all reserve tins out of private tin stores. I have only 1 marg. and 1 cond. milk in store. All parcels to be moved outside the camp. Had hair cut in aft. Read in evening. Fathomed out present worth and discount (True and Practical) with Paddy after afternoon tea.

18 October. New arrivals due, but only 3 turned up so far. ARA in morn. Read in morning. Walked round with Ray C. after tea. ARA before tea. Rain in morning, but a little sun in aft. Went to Rum Pot with Bert Ash. Paddy had taken the place of the guitarist, although he did not even know the tunes!! He did OK! ARA after 'Ginger Snaps' and dark journey back!! AA and bombing to the NW while we were going over. V. quick!! ARA again v. late at night.

19 October. Dull day with rain at times. Read in morning. Letters from Daddy dated 23 Aug and Peter d 21 Aug. News that 140 boys now at Rishworth. Spent some time in library in aft. and then walked round with Paddy. C.B. said that his mother had seen CSM Miles in England. Stevens came back from Bruns. Hospital. He said that it was a miracle the hospital was not hit in the raid, that the town was blazing around it, that Butler-Shaw was too ill to be moved and that his ward (top one) caught alight from incendiaries, but our 2 orderlies put the fire out and won praise from the Germans. The other patients spent 12 hours in the cellars, which rocked like a ship during the raid – in fact, indescribable terror in Brunswick and hospital. Distributed tin store stocks in morning. Went to Rum Pot again in evening. ARA (yellow) interrupted the floor show, which was almost finished.

20 October. Quite sunny in morning. Walked round. Read

a bit. Talked to Blackie in aft. News of American landing in Philippines. Over 100 new arrivals in evening (Arnhem). Wrote P.C. home (No 84).

☆ ☆ ☆

22 October. Went to Communion and Matins (United Services). Finished reading French book. V. interesting. 2 ARAs in afternoon from 1.20 to 4.00 with short break for tea!! V. heavy AA once, and planes over twice. V. low cloud, so could not see bombers. Went to shelter twice for short time. Big fire raging somewhere SE of Brunswick (saw it in evening). Went to Symphony Concert before roll call – v.g. programme, including Beethoven's 5th Symphony, Mozart's Overture to *The Marriage of Figaro,* march from *Tannhaüser* (Wagner), and another Mozart piece. ARA in evening. (Water sometimes comes on in this house for an hour in afternoon; but cannot use 'lats' yet, as drains not complete – French 'Commando' (ie working party) working on them and the steam pipes. Water not 'on' so much now since night raid!) Brunswick town also bombed in aft. – big explosion. ARA in the night, but did not wake up. Beat Jim Alp at chess in evening.

☆ ☆ ☆

23 October. Specimen menus – yesterday: Can. coffee; millet; tea; fried meat roll and pots with tea – today: Can. coffee; pots hot water; tea; German stew and G coffee for breakfast, lunch, tea and dinner respectively – all being v. small rations.
24 October. Letter dated 1 June (in envelope dated 7 July) from Aline. Read during day. Dried cabbage soup for lunch – awful!! ARA for 2 hours in aft. Bombers heard but not seen due to low dense cloud. AA and several low-flying planes machine-gunned aerodrome and/or autobahn and railway. Went to shelter twice for short time. ARA in evening, and lights off most of time.

☆ ☆ ☆

26 October. 2nd Anniversary of becoming POW!! Wrote L/C (No 85) home. Big washing day in aft.!! Washed 2 prs of pants,

2 vests, 1 shirt, 1 towel, 1 pr socks, 1 pillow case, 1 pr pyjama trousers and 7 handkerchiefs. Waited some time for electricity to come on before washing most of them. 1 hours ARA in aft! Played Roy twice at chess in even. 1st game was 'stalemate', as he could keep putting me in check although I was well 'up' on pieces. I won second game.

27 October. Cold dull day – as usual. Commandant granted us our system of mail distribution! Read during day. Spent some time in Toc H room. No hope of drying my washing!! News that Archbishop of York (Temple) had died of a heart attack – a great pity, as he would have been ideal for post-war Britain, with his moderate political opinions and his hopes of a reunion of the churches. ARA after 'lights out' and again in the early hours of morning. Planes overhead especially the second time. Distant AA both times?

☆ ☆ ☆

1 November. Cloudy day. Rainy to start with (indoor roll call), but 'peep' of sun later on. Got up early (ie 8.00 am!!) to have a cold shower. Water 'on' only in houses 5 and 7: – our house's drains have been repaired for about 10 days now, but Brunswick water supply has been dislocated since big night raid on 14 October. (Steam pipes damaged on 24 August are still not yet repaired, though a French commando team have been working on the crater for some time now.) ARA in morning. Read *The Countryman* and my book in Toc H Room in morning. Chatted to Andy in aft, and Jim, Wilf and I went to Rum Pot (new programme) in evening. Only saw the first turn in the Floor Show – 'The Harmony Fumf' (with 'Banjo' Watson) which was excellent and kept us roaring with laughter. ARA then stopped 'play'.

2 November. Finished reading Buchan's *Montrose* – excellent account of a fine figure. V. good description of the current state of affairs and of the condition of Scotland. Got *The Close of the Middle Ages* (1272-1494) by R. Lodge out of Educational library. Sunny day with cloud cover. 2 hours ARA. Hundreds and hundreds of planes passed over to the south, going westwards. Distant bombing to the south. Many fighters stooging about during alert – some quite low. Went to shelters twice for a short time – the second time with Jim Alp when a big AA barrage opened up on a single plane (probably in trouble) which had strayed over the camp from a second batch of bombers to the south. We (in shelters) thought it was bombing. Sudden AA during lunch made us 'do a recce', but it was only fighters. Walked round with Bob during the afternoon. No electricity during day, so could not read in late aft. Roll call (as yesterday and henceforth) at 6.00 pm inside. ARA after the meal. Isolated planes over. One bang (distant bomb?). Wrote P.C. (No 86) home.

3 November. Dull and cold day. Read 100 pages of new book. Went to Rum Pot in evening, but 'yellow' alarm after second cabaret turn ('Swiss Family Wittlebot'). (Water supply still chronic, and only 'on' in houses 5 and 7 at intervals.)

4 November. Was room orderly offr. Dull and cloudy. Read a bit during day. Long ARA in morning. Hundreds of planes passed to the north going westwards. Markers in direction of Hanover, and some people saw smoke in that direction after the raid. Fighters and planes all over the place, and went to shelter for short time when bombs fell – because, as soon as one looked one way, planes came the other side!! ARA in evening. Flares, flashes, ARA and rumbling of bombs to the west. Beat Roy at chess in evening.

☆ ☆ ☆

13 November. Political theory lecture in morning – dealing with the rise of Nation States, Machiavelli and Discovery of New World, Theories of Divine Right and Social Contract, Hobbes and Locke and Rousseau. Read after the lecture. Went to discussion in the aft. on 'Post-War Army?' – Major Forbes spoke on regular army, Capt Green on TA, Major Taylor on the Reg army and Major Macheil on the Canadian army. Taylor recommended the supremacy of the RAF in a combined staff, RAF Regts to be extended to AA etc, and to do overseas garrison duties aided by local native police, and a powerful striking force on the form of machines (eg tanks, guns, heavy mortars and planes) rather than manpower, which would be highly trained in all the latest weapons and would not cost more than pre-war infantry force. In the following discussion, an Aussie (Ordish) advocated the training of British Units in Australia and other Dominions in order to get to know one another better (and vice versa). Very interesting. Read in new Silence Room in basement of House 1 after tea. Water situation chronic – very cold using outside latrines!! Read in evening. No ARAs!! Froze at night.

15 November. Thin coating of snow on ground in morning. Read in basement of house 1 in morning. Central heating came on for a time in the morning and in evening. Went to *School for Scandal* (Sheridan) in afternoon produced by Alastair Bannerman. The first act was rather rotten, but enjoyed the last two acts after tea. Good acting and excellent costumes. ARA in evening. An odd spot of AA when at the latrines. Wrote P.C. (No 88) home. About 18 new arrivals arrived in evening – captured 3 weeks ago. Stitched battle-dress trousers up, as I had torn them.

17 November. Went to lecture by Solomons on the 'National Capital' in economics series. Read afterwards. Heated water up in aft. for a 'wash-bath', shaved, cleaned shoes and put my collar and tie on – just a practice for going home!! Went to German newsreel on the 'Invasion' quite good, but where was the invasion?!! Sun came out during day. Heating on for short time in early morning and evening. Wilf and I beat Tony and Jock at bridge in evening. Wrote L/C (No 89) home. Dick Lishmund mended my pullover, as it had frayed at the sleeve (short-sleeved). Johnny Hall gave me 10 Players.

22 November. Read *The Londoner* by Lady Dorothy Nicholson in 'British People in Pictures' series in morning. Read and dozed for a bit in aft. A recent arrival said that the bombing of this camp had been brought up by the Minister of Air in the House of Commons!! 5 more new arrivals today. Bob and I had pilchards on toast and chips in evening. Rainy day. (Went to lecture in aft. on Post-War Government: 'Medical Services'.)

23 November. Political theory talk on Presidents of the old German Republic and the USA, and the beginning of the 'legislature' with particular reference to the House of Lords. Read afterwards. Washed pyjamas and a towel in aft. Jock and I beat Listerson and partner by 1,400 points at bridge after tea. Bob and I had egg and potato omelette at night – meal in dark. 2 ARAs and lights off most of evening.

24 November. Economic lecture on distribution of National Capital, and introduction to National Income. Read in morning and received library book. Pancakes for tea. Bob's Gurkha brought him some curry. Germans admitted fighting in Strasbourg. 'Curried bread and potato' in evening!! ARA. Bombing in Hanover area and planes overhead. Beat Roy at chess. Bob and I ate creamed rice in evening, although we originally intended to have it on Monday!! Water on in our house for the night.

☆　☆　☆

26 November. Sunny day, but much colder especially the wind. Went to Communion. Walked round with Andy and Blackie, and went to Matins with latter – cut short due to ARA. Watched the raid on Hanover area for rest of morning. 36 waves passed over to the north of the camp, and dropped markers and bombs on Hanover area. Could hear loud rumbles. Watched from attic of 2L for some time. Saw AA tracer going up, but very little AA considering. Read during aft. and evening. 'German stew' for dinner; 'fried' chips (not much fat!!). Bob and I peeled potato peels in evening!! ARA in night. Very cold night – frost.

27 November. No bread issue all day. Also, no sugar which was due last Monday. Went to political theory lecture in morning – from Rousseau and Bentham's Utilitarianism to Idealism, Individualism, 3 schools of Unreason and Hagelianism. Peeled more 'peels' in morning, and then boiled the results. ARA at midday – formations of fighters and AA overhead, but I missed it (cooking). Went to debate on League of Nations – Benharan for, and Ackroyd against. Left before the latter finished speaking, as I was on a path-making party. However, only a few tools turned up and the hand-cart was broken, so our room was not wanted!! Drew English parcel in aft. Bob and I went to 3 German short films on Bison and Fujiama (Japan) in aft. Very poor. Very cold day, but sunny. Bob and I had sausages and peas for dinner. Very good!!. No lights from roll call till nearly lights-out apart from short interval. 2 ARAs and loud explosion in second!! – apparently the flash was at least 2 miles to the west. Froze at night.

6 December. Read most of day. Hard ground and sunny day after last night's frost. 2 hours ARA in morning and early afternoon – distant bombing, AA and fighters seen. Egg omelette for dinner. Lights out all evening (ARA). Bombing in Hanover direction, followed by AA and bombing south of Brunswick including a big flash. Brewed hot water for cocoa.* (Cannot use 'We've got it's' (code word for heaters) now!! ie. till Sat. and then not in evening.)

10 December. Very dark and miserable day – lights off all day. Went to Matins. Bob cooked potato 'cakes' for lunch. I peeled 'peelings' before church. Read after lunch. Visited Blackie after tea – also Sadler from 1/5 Queens who was recently taken POW in Holland. He said that Borrett and Russell Elliott had been killed in Normandy. German stew for dinner. Very 'fed up'!! – but unfortunately only in one sense!! Froze at night. Slight snow. Made cocoa in evening.

11 December. Bob and I went 'wood-foraging'!! Political theory lecture on Communism (1st, 2nd and 3rd International). Cooked spud peelings for lunch. Read in aft. Letter dated 25 October from Aline – news that Margie's American friend 'Pep' was not at all a success with family, but Margie 'more determined to stick by him'!! Hugh Nugent married 3 weeks ago. Went to 'Radio Croce Rossa' with Tommy Sampson's band in afternoon – not very good. Can parcel issue. Sardines on toast and potato 'cakes' (and Sauerkraut) in

---

* There were home-made immersion heaters, but when electricity off we used 'STUFAS' fired with brush to brew up. The former were later forbidden when the Germans found out.

evening. 2 ARAs in evening – bombing in Hanover direction. Brewed water for cocoa. Wrote L/C (No 93) home in evening.

12 December. Made two puddings in morning. 'Beer' issue. Potato cakes for lunch. Went to talk on Australia by Guest in afternoon – mainly on history. Curried salmon in evening. ARA at midday, and 2 more in evening (rumbles in Hanover area). Brewed water for cocoa in evening. Finished reading Acton's *Lectures on Modern History* – excellent book and well worth re-reading.

15 December. Froze during day. Still no lights during day – telegram sent to Protecting Power. Prepared 'bully and pot' pie for baking – had it for dinner. Read in morning and early afternoon. ARA – bombing and AA south of Brunswick (lunchtime). Brewed coffee for lunch. Lecture on 'France – before and after the war' by a Frenchman in afternoon – excellent talk. A 'lame major' and I beat Roy and George Marrs by 1,800 points in evening – should have won by more, but the major bid 3-card suits etc!! ARA after evening meal – very distant rumbles. (Pen nib just about 'kaput'.)

16 December. Read in Toc H Room in morning. Letter d 5 November from Mum – news that Margie was at Newcastle; also mentions Xmas parcels (and still hope!!). Read in early afternoon and evening. Inoculated for typhus in afternoon. Cooked potato cakes and fried 'pudding' for dinner. Thawed in evening, but froze at night.

18 December. Even better than usual political theory talk on Communism in Russia and Fascism. Reading during day. ARA at lunchtime. Drew Canadian parcel in afternoon. German stew for dinner. ARA in evening and 'yellow' later on. Tony and I lost by 1,800 points to Bob and Paddy in evening. Dennis Butler-Shaw returned from Brunswick Hospital – quite cheerful, but his remaining leg and body very thin. News that German counter-offensive started at 0530 hours on the 16th north of Luxembourg! Wrote P.C. (No 95) home.

☆ ☆ ☆

20 December. Was room stooge. Went to 'Xmas Pie' in afternoon for an hour – music and variety by Willy Wilshaw in Rum Pot annex. Tony Jacobs and I lost by 2,100 points in evening. Fish cakes for dinner. (Bratling soup for lunch). Germans claimed 10,000 prisoners, 200 tanks (incl. 'captured') in USA 1st Army Sector!! Very cold night.

21 December. Political theory lecture on the connections between the legislature, executive and judiciary (cabinet etc.) Prepared salmon and potatoes for steaming (tin salmon between two). Read a bit. Washed all and peeled some potato peelings. Received 500 Players from Mrs J.A. Sharp pp. Grove Park School, and 200 Players from Ripponden Comforts – very welcome indeed, especially as yesterday's cig issue of 15 was the last. Definite news that 2,500 food parcels on the way – hope they are Xmas ones. Bob cooked chips and I fried up half a pudding – these with the salmon pie were very satisfying!! Tony and I were 4,600 up at bridge in evening. Germans claimed 20,000 prisoners altogether now!! – also to have crossed Liege-Bartogue-Arlon road in their counter-offensive. Very cold day – heating not on properly. Froze hard at night.

22 December. Water not on first thing in morning. Froze all day. Peeled and cooked spud peelings in morning. Tried without success to get tea for cigs at Exchange and Mart. Went to tea with C.B. Helped Wilf to make Xmas decorations. Fried meat roll cakes for dinner. Read in evening. Had cold shower in evening.

23 December. Made Xmas pudding in morning – 3 Canadian biscuits, a little bread, packet raisins. packet prunes plus kernels, mug of beer, and a lot of sugar and margarine. Canadian parcel issue instead of on Monday – also bread issue. Letter d. 6 November from Daddy. Very cold day and night. Prepared bully and potatoes for steaming for dinner. Helped Wilf put Xmas decorations up in afternoon. Duncan painted holly etc. on the wall. Read a bit in evening. Inoculated (for typhus) in afternoon. Yesterday I wrote P.C. to Mrs Sharp. 2 yellow alarms this morning, and both a red and a yellow in evening.

24 December. Spent some time tying pudding up – two

Klim tin rims broke!! Went to Matins with Blackie. Letter dated 29 October from Mum – news that Peter confirmed at Rossall on 30 November. ARA in afternoon and 'yellow' in evening. Went to Carol Service after tea in attic of House 2 – very good, but very cold feet!! Choir sang well and so did we!! Cold bully and potatoes for dinner. Very cold day!! – ground as hard as iron. Crushed biscuits for tomorrow's porridge in early afternoon and prepared tomorrow's lunch in evening. Went to see Room 47's cake. Heating very poor in our room. Choir came round the buildings in evening and sang carols. Gramophone in our room at night. Talked to George Marrs in evening. Brewed coffee after 11.00 pm, and went to midnight Sung Eucharist at 11.45 – only just got in, and a big queue turned away. Over 300 present. Into bed after 1.00 am – 'Lights Out' concession from Commandant.

25 December. CHRISTMAS DAY. No roll calls during the day (the SBO had given parole). Got up for coffee at 9.00. John and I cooked breakfast, ie biscuit porridge with prunes, raisins, Klim etc. in it, sardines on toast; toast and marmalade; and tea – Bob and Jim got up in time to eat it! Went to Matins in attic of House 5 (ie cinema) but rather cold. Sunny day, but freezing! Band played carols round the camp. Heating very bad as usual in our room. (Yesterday, we had Christmas messages from the SBO; Maj Gen Sir Richard Howard-Vyse (Chairman of POW Dept of British Red X), Mr Mackenzie King (PM of Canada) and a very sweet one from the Queen). Pea soup, fried Canadian pork roll and chips, slice of bread, and tea for lunch – Bob and I gave away pieces of meat roll and chips (which the mess had prepared excellently) as we were so full!! Also ate some chocolate! Roy had given us all 20 British Consols and Wilf gave us a bar of chocolate between two. Jim and I walked for an hour in aft; the first exercise for weeks!! Felt warmer during the day – in fact, ever since last night's communion service when my feet thawed for the first time for two days. Consequently my chilblains are a bit sore underfoot. Prepared tonight's curried salmon before tea. A few visitors to tea – tables lengthwise and together, and Xmas tree in middle. Had a Canadian biscuit split in half with cheese and marmalade on. Also two slices of Duncan's and Bob's cakes!! Visited Andy in afternoon and strolled about with him for a bit. Cooked curried salmon and toast for Bob,

Jim and me before dinner. Bob and I saved some of our German stew, ate all our salmon and were stumped after a few mouthfuls of Xmas pudding and Klim sauce! The pudding was excellent and very well cooked. The mess have done wonderfully with the cooking. Also had coffee and 'beer'. In agony afterwards!! – stomach almost bursting!! – twice to the lavatory to date (9.30 pm)!! Visited Rum Pot for quarter of an hour in evening. Wrote L/C (No 96) home. Had an excellent day and wonderful spirit in camp.

26 December. BOXING DAY. Not so full this morning, but not so hungry as usual!! Finished pudding off during day, and Bob and I warmed up half of yesterday's German stew for lunch. Went back to bed after roll call! Freezing day as usual. Heating did not work in morning, but did in the afternoon, when the Commandant and a General came round!! Blackie cut my hair, and stayed to tea in the afternoon. Made a small pudding in evening! (A day or two ago, the Germans said in their communique that Manchester had been bombarded by their long-range weapons.)

27 December. Sunny but freezing day. Finished reading *Henry VII* – not very good book. Started reading Lipson's *Europe in the 19th Century.* Washed 8 hankies, 2 pairs of socks, a balaclava, pyjama jacket and short-sleeved pullover – in ice-cold water!! Had hot shower after dinner (7.30 pm) – the 2nd since last spring! Caught two mice in our room in evening. Paddy drowned the first, and I let the other one escape when I was trying to drown it!! Bully pie (1/3 tin) for dinner. Brewed tea for lunch, and in evening. Made brew in evening. Jim and Duncan got next-of-kin parcel (chocs).

28 December. 'Yellow' in early morning. Roll call when it was snowing. Back to bed!! Bob and I booked a meal out at the Rum Pot for next Tuesday. Tried to read in the afternoon, but too cold to concentrate. 2/3 tin of bully for lunch (B and I), and German stew for dinner. ARA in evening. Jim, John, Ray and I went to Camp Coffee Pot in basement 2 in evening – good cup of tea and very cosy room. Fuel shortage in cookhouse – no steaming etc. till further notice.

29 December. Back to bed, and read a bit. Heating not on – Assistant Commandant came into room. 2,500 Eng parcels arrived in camp – thank goodness! Very cold day as usual – misty. Went to Marionette show in hospital after tea. Sardines for dinner. Jim, John and I went to Camp Coffee Pot in evening. Wrote P.C. (No 97) home. Yellow alarms in morning and evening.

30 December. Stayed in bed after roll call. Read a bit. 4,000 Canadian parcels arrived. Eng parcel issue instead of on New Year's Day. Snowed during day. 3rd inoculation (typhus) in afternoon – stung like a wasp!! Fried bread and meat roll for dinner. Bert and I visited 2L in evening!! Brewed coffee in evening! Several ARAs and yellows during day, and lights off all evening practically. German treacle issue.

31 December. Was Room Orderly Officer. Beer issue in morning. Went to Matins but ARA cut it short before the sermon. Bombing to the north and in Hanover direction. Saw markers over Hanover – pall of smoke on horizon. Sunny day – snow on the ground and freezing. Read in afternoon. Fried meat roll (tin) and fried bread for dinner – 'bashed' a lot of tomorrow's bread ration which we got yesterday!! 'Yellow' in afternoon and ARA in evening – planes (goon?) heard, and bombing (?). Jim, John, Bert and I went to 'Coffee Pot' for tea, when lights came on. Afterwards, we could not get into Rum Pot (crammed full). Brewed cocoa at night. Saw the New Year in in bed!! Good riddance to the Old One!! Jim, Bob, Wilf, Paddy and I formed an anti-swearing league – 1 cig for offence!!

1945

1 January. NEW YEAR'S DAY. Stayed in bed most of morning. Bob and I took food to Rum Pot for our meal tomorrow. Sunny day, but freezing and snow on ground. Saw 3 big formations of bombers drop flares and bombs to the NE (7-10 miles?) – markers also dropped in Hanover area and to the NNW. Scores of fighters weaving about. Clouds of silver paper dropped. Read in afternoon. German stew for dinner, and creamed rice for lunch. 'Yellow' in afternoon and ARA at night. Brewed up in evening and morning.

2 January. ARA in morn. Stayed in bed and read till lunch (pea soup). Letter dated 9 October from Mum. She had received my P.C. dated 30 July re 'Hailing' (Heil Hitler after bomb plot). Bob and I went to Rum Pot in evening. Lights out at first, due to ARA. We then had a 3-course meal – potato with thick salmon sauce on; potato with sweet curried bully; and a pudding with a sweet sauce – also coffee and sugar. Very tasty and piping hot. Cost 64 'bully marks' ie 1 slab of chocolate (30), 1 salmon (15), 2 slices of bread (4) and 15 potatoes. Tom Russell and a friend of his joined us over our coffee. Tommy Sampson's cabaret and full band also Pitso's orchestra, 3 cabaret turns: Howson dressed up as a Sikh, Louis Geduld and Tom Meehan in a silent 'fish and chip' scene, and Paul Hardwicke as a parson. Very enjoyable.

3 January. Finished reading *Europe in the 19th Century* by Lipson – very concise and clear picture of European affairs. Stayed in bed after roll call. Drizzled and thawed during day. Heating quite good in afternoon (due to increased pressure for showers in hospital block?). More rumours of new arrivals, supposed to be Americans – the latest is that the camp is beng extended to hold an extra 3,000!! Got *A History of the Vikings* by T.D. Kendrick out of Educational library. Went to 'Scrapbook

for 1944' in Rum Pot annex after tea with T. Sampson's band and a resume of the less important events of last year – surprisingly good. Cooked a stew in even. – the ingredients were 1 tin of cottage pie (plenty of suet in it), a spoonful of Yorkshire pudding mixture, ration of turnips, 1 tin of peas and potatoes. Very good!! Tony and I lost by 1,200 points to 'Ham' and Tom Vincent in evening. Brewed cocoa before going to bed.

5 January. Letter dated 10 August from Margie. In bed till lunch as usual. Sheets of ice on ground after last night's frost. 'Yellow' at lunch. Washed some peelings and some bits of curly kale in afternoon. Went to *Meet the Stewarts* after tea – an American film with Francis Dee and William Holden in it. Very enjoyable and amusing, although a second-rate film. Cooked some pancakes for dinner (tin egg powder, 3/4 pkt Yorkshire pudding and some flour). ARA afterwards – bombing and flashes to the west and planes overhead. Several of us went to the Coffee Pot, but it was closed! Brewed cocoa. ARA again later – flashes and planes overhead.

8 January. Stayed in bed and read a bit, after an indoor roll call (the first for weeks or months). Snow on ground (few inches). Barley for lunch. Canadian parcel issue in afternoon. Sam Sturgeon newly arrived and moved into our room – he had been captured in December when Germans were pushed back over the Maas. Went to the Pantomime *Aladdin* with Tom Meehan, Louis Geduld, Paul Hardwicke, Alan Glover, Tony Watson, Peter Brewin etc in it. Excellent show – I think the best I have seen in the bag! One laugh from start to finish; popular tunes from the orchestra and excellently produced. 'Props' wonderful. Not very cold in theatre apart from my feet. Cold sardines for dinner. Divided parcel with Bob Melville who was moving to warmer room (46). Gordon moved to 45, and Roy and I moved to House 1 room 19. I am sharing with Bert Ash now (with Wilf and Paddy). Cleaned cupboard out etc. Crushed a biscuit each for 3 of us (for porridge). Washed a filthy German towel. Paddy made a brew in evening. Sewed button on in evening.

☆ ☆ ☆

12 January. Read in bed for most of morning. Barley for lunch. Letter dated 1 October from Dad. Started to thaw. Read most of day. Fried meat roll, potatoes, turnips and pudding for dinner. Usual brews (tea at lunch, and cocoa in evening).

13 January. Went back to bed as usual and read. P.C. (wishing Happy Xmas) from Mum. Notified that I have a cig parcel tomorrow. Walked round with Andy after tea. Started to freeze again. News that Russians began offensive on Vistula bridge-head at Baranov, and activity in East Prussia. Jock and I beat Tony and John Williams by 4,400 points at bridge in evening. Bought some tea for cigarettes. Fried meat roll for lunch, and bully stew for dinner (from mess).

14 January. Did not wake up in time for Communion. Biscuit porridge for breakfast. Collected 200 Craven A from parcel store (from Uncle C dated 13/7/44). Went to Matins and stayed for Communion afterwards. 'Yellow' alarm during service. Pea soup for lunch. Red alarm from about 1.00 till 2.20. Heavy AA and markers over Brunswick direction (other side of town) and bombing. Then a formation turned towards here and passed over the camp, then turning in a north-westerly direction, but I did not see the latter turn as I had gone to shelter for a minute or two. (1st time for months!!) Later on, 4 big waves bombed to the NE (3 miles away?). Saw markers. Perfect sky, and sun – still freezing. Bags of fighters zooming about all over the place. More AA and bombing to the SW (Bruns. direction). The camp shook, and bombing loud. Could see nothing from attics owing to ground mist. Read a bit after tea. Cooked fishcakes (1 tin salmon) for dinner (very good), turnips from mess, and Bert Ash made an excellent 'sweet' (1 Can. biscuits, prunes, Klim and a few raisins). Jock and I beat Paddy and Tony by about 1,000 points at bridge in even; and then long ARA stopped play – planes overhead and flashes in Brunswick direction (?). Usual brews for lunch and in evening. Long ARA after 'Lights Out' – prolonged drone of planes after 'yellow' on return from

Berlin.

16 January. Finished reading *A History of the Vikings* in bed. Letter from Aline dated 25 August. 'Yellow' and 'red' warnings during morning. Low cloud prevented 'visibility'. Formations of planes overhead and I went to the shelter for a minute when AA opened up. Two more 'yellows' lasted most of afternoon. Went to lecture on 'Applied Economics', introduction – very poor lecture. Washed 11 hankies and the collar and sleeves of my battle-dress after tea. Pea soup for lunch; and fish cakes (salmon (between 2) which I cooked) and sauerkraut for dinner. Usual lunch and evening brews. Got *Captain Paul* by Commander Edward Elleberg out of library. 'Yellow' in evening and lights out; followed after a short 'all clear' by an ARA. Roar of bomber formations continued for almost an hour, flares to the south, a red flare to the north. Ack Ack (fairly distant but audible at times), flashed all round but especially to the east (Magdeburg) where there was a terrific 'party', the flashes lit up innumerable vapour trails in the sky to the NE, and judging from the roar of planes I should think that it was one of the biggest forces to pass over this neighbourhood. A few searchlights also up, and a few explosions, and rumbles heard. Very clear night, but no moon.

☆ ☆ ☆

19 January. Biscuits (soaked), prunes and Klim for breakfast. Read in bed after roll call. Rain, sleet and snow most of day. Cooked turnip peelings in afternoon and chopped wood. Went to 'Operetta' in Rum Pot annex after tea. Unfortunately the lights went on and off most of time, and after a late start we had two more interruptions, so I went out before the end – quite good programme including excerpts from *Tom Jones* and 'Lilac Time' by the choir. Bert and I cooked fried bully and turnips, chips, fried bread and toast for dinner. Tony and I beat Jock and Paddy by 400 points at bridge in the evening – dull cards all round. Brewed up at lunch and in evening for our syndicate. Froze at night.

20 January. Sun shone most of day. 'Yellow' alarm in morning. Read in bed. Letter dated 1 October from M. (News that Aline's 'special friend' Junior had been killed. Also news of 'Black-out' restrictions being removed.) Heated turnip up to add to pea soup for lunch. Wrote L/C (No 100) home in afternoon. Also prepared meat roll 'cakes' for dinner. Went to lecture by Jean Anlois in French on 'La Pacification de l'Afrique du Nord' – understood most of it, surprisingly!! Very brief account of the acquisition of France's N. African Empire. Cooked meat roll cakes and fried bread for dinner. Very good! Paddy and I beat Tony and Jock by 3,100 points at bridge in evening.

22 January. Was room stooge. Letter dated 22 October from Mum. News that the 'POW Magazine said that Oflag 79 could not be considered a safe distance from the town and bombing.' (!!) Beer issue. Read a bit in morning. 2 'Yellow' alarms. Pea soup for lunch. Ackroyd's *Growth of Parliamentary Government* series in afternoon (from the Tudor despotism to the Restoration). Parcel issue (Eng) a good one, including butter and bacon. Went to debate after tea – 29-7 against the present constitution of the House of Lords. Cheese and potatoes for dinner – as we had a lot of bread and biscuits today. Cocoa instead of tea for evening brew. ARA in evening. Read afterwards. (Started a cold a few days ago, but threw it off before it developed.)

25 January. Very cold day. Finished reading *Captain Paul* – very good book. Got *The Origin and Growth of Greater Britain* by Hugh Edward Egerton out of Educational library – an introduction to Colonial history. Cooked fried bread and toast cheese for lunch. Went to Chris Ackroyd's lecture on 'The State' in afternoon, and then to Lt J.L.H. Coup de Frejac's lecture in French on 'The Educational System in France' – understood the general trend (difference between English and French systems: 'Education' and 'instruction', 'culture as an end' and 'culture as a means' etc.). German stew for dinner. George Marrs came for a chat in evening. Bert and I 'foraged' for fuel.

26 January. Very cold day – fine snow falling. Cooked porridge oats in morning. Read. Wrote L/C (No 101) home. (27 American officers arrived a few days ago after being bombed badly at a transit camp 300 yds from Limburg marshalling yards.) Heavy fall of snow during day. Made English meat roll 'cakes' after lunch. Went to 'Roll on the Day' after tea – rather poor variety, but music, David Buchanan, and Howson (Italian Sergeant) were very good. Cooked rissoles and peas for dinner. George and I beat the two majors in his room by 2,700 points at bridge in evening.

☆　☆　☆

1 February. Roll call outside despite slushy snow and water lying on ground. Thawing fast and nearly all snow finished during day. Was room stooge. Read a bit during day. Wrote P.C. (No 102) home and to Bradley. Had letter dated 7 December from Bradley. News that he had been married 18 months! Went to lecture by Ackroyd on the 'End' of the State and the question of 'Obedience' to the State – very good lecture as usual. Barley for lunch. Cooked (after having prepared) 'chopped ham' (or spam) cakes for dinner, and heated tinned carrots up. Germans admitted that the Russians had reached the Oder NE of Berlin. Long ARA in evening. Planes overhead and flashes including flares to the north.

2 February. ARA in early hours of morning. Got up for a second (as did all the room!) and an odd 'bang'. A few planes heard, but many heard later on the way back (when I was asleep). Stayed in bed after roll call. Read all day. 4 'Yellows' during morning (including an odd and sudden Ack Ack burst). Cooked fish-cakes for lunch (plus turnips from mess). Got *England Under the Stuarts* by G.M. Trevelyan out of Educational library, but did not start it, as had not finished other book yet. M and V stew from mess for dinner. ARA all evening. Planes overhead. Brewed up for Bert in evening. Windy, but quite mild day – snow gone.

3 February. ARA during morning. AA (and bombing?). Planes heard. Overcast day. Windy and coldish. Read most of the day. Two 'Yellows' in afternoon, and ARA during dinner.

Bacon pie for dinner.

4 February. Went to Communion and Matins. Finished reading *John Pym* – quite good. Started reading Trevelyan's *England Under the Stuarts* in Sir Charles Oman's series of 'History of England'. Read *The Spectator* (camp newspaper) in afternoon, and visited Andy and Blackie. After a frost last night, sleet and rain fell during day. Brewed up for lunch and also fried spam, bread and potatoes. Paddy and I beat Tom Vincent and Ham by 1,300 points after 3 games of bridge in evening, before the lights went out – ARA and distant 'crumps'. Brewed up in evening. Drew pillow and bed cover in a cut of the cards, as a few came into camp today. Good German stew for dinner.

7 February. Dull day, slight drizzle. Read a bit during day. Gramophone in room, but it did not work. Iggulden's lecture in afternoon on the Uthwatt Committee's Report on Land Nationalization. ARA and lights out all evening. Planes overhead. Barley with chocolate, raisins and prunes in it (these came out of damaged Canadian parcels) – for lunch. Salmon pie for dinner. No brew in evening (run out of cocoa). Another ARA after lights out, but I was asleep.

9 February. Read in bed in morning. 'Turnip Soup' (water?) for lunch. ARA from 10.00 till 2.00 (distant bombings of Brunswick?) Red X representative visited camp. Could not speak English!! Read during day. Made and cooked fish-cakes for dinner. Also had big pudding. Paddy and I continued bridge – 1,300 points up at end.

11 February. Went to Matins. Prepared meat roll 'cakes' for tonight. About 3 'Yellows' in morning. Was room stooge. Quite sunny day. Read in afternoon. Paddy and I lost by 500 points to Jock and Tony in evening. Brewed up for afternoon tea. Swapped Canadian butter (tomorrow) for one ounce of

109

Players tobacco, and had my first cig for several days. Cooked the meat roll 'cakes' for dinner, but they fell to bits! – too runny. (Another 1,000 of the cigs stolen from the store the other day were found in the basement of house 2L. The first 1,000 were found in the attic yesterday.) Filled water-butt in 'lats'. Sprinkling of snow at night.

12 February. Read in bed in morning. Brewed up and cooked sardines on toast for lunch. Went to Ackroyd's lecture on Parliamentary Government under the first two Georges. Drew ½ Canadian parcel – the last of our stock! Read after tea. Paddy and I lost by 500 points again at bridge in evening. Morale up!! – Russians on move again (West of Breslau) and the Western front 'developing' promisingly!! German stew for dinner. ARA after 'lights out' – woke up when a 'bang' startled everyone – very heavy bombs later on shook the buildings. Rained hard during night.

13 February. 2 'Yellows' in morning. Read in bed. Wrote L/C (No 103) home. Read most of the fortnight's issue of *The Spectator* (a wall newspaper) in afternoon. Also read the 'Camp'. Put my name down for the *Oflag 79 Anthology* to be sent to me after the war. Had stomach ache in evening!! Cold meat roll, sauerkraut and boiled potatoes for dinner. Jock and I were beating Will Wilshaw and Carfray by 1,500 points at bridge in evening, when the ARA went – planes overhead. Another ARA later on woke me up – continuous drone of planes and several 'odd bombs' (some quite close which shook buildings). Rained at night, but as usual had stopped by tomorrow morning's roll call!!

15 February. Finished reading *England Under the Stuarts* by Trevelyan. Very excellent book on the period and worth a detailed study in the future. Finished making out genealogical tables of the Stuarts and the Spanish Succession. Prepared fish cakes for tonight. Long ARA in morning – distant AA. Barley (or some smaller cereal?) for lunch. 'Yellow' in afternoon. Went to Ackroyd's lecture on the three essential *rights* of Democracy ie. liberty (political, civil and individual), Equality (anti-exploitation) and Fraternity (welfare of society). Very good lecture as usual. Got a short biography of *William of*

Orange by G.J. Reneir out of library. Sunny afternoon. Went to 'Night Ride' in afternoon – a programme of 'Round the London dance bands ten years ago' with Tommy Sampson's band, The band was excellent as also were impersonations of Flanagan and Allen, Bob Hope and the Mills Brothers. News that a consignment of 1,500 parcels have been sent off (on the 10th). Paddy and I lost by 500 points at bridge in evening. Cooked fish cakes for dinner – also had turnips (as usual) and a pudding. Gave 150 marks (£10) to become a Founder and Life Member of the proposed 'Brunswick Boys' Club'. Very clear night. No ARAs.

17 February. Read in bed in morning. Gongs on sentry boxes sounded for extra roll call in morning – after a lapse of time the SBO had the bugle sounded, and we then fell in in the corridors!! Pea soup for lunch. Prepared tonight's salmon pie before lunch, and put dried (hard) garlic in it. Finished reading *William of Orange* – quite interesting but short. Got *Bishop Burnett's History of His Own Times* out of library. Salmon pie and a pudding, plus sauerkraut and spuds for dinner – good meal. Paddy and I drew with Tony and Jock in evening. Short ARA in evening. 'Yellow' at lunch time. Radiators not on till 5.00 pm and then only for short time. Sunny day, but very cold without heating (due to general shortage of coal. Henceforth, heaters not to be on in the 'forenoon' when it is 'mild').

18 February. Did not wake up for Communion. Went to Matins. Visited Andy and Blackie beforehand. Misty and damp morning. Big 'laundry' day in afternoon!! – washed 2 shirts, 2 vests, 2 pairs of pants, 2 pairs of socks and 6 hankies, 1 towel and 1 pair of pyjama trousers. Very cold and unpleasant job. Last bit of Red X soap. Had cold meat roll, turnips and potatoes for lunch. German stew for dinner. Heaters not on at all during the day. News that Spittal bombed by two fortresses last autumn – 60 (including 20 British) killed. Also news of cut in German ration for tomorrow. The cuts are shown in the column on the right:

	per week	cut to
potatoes	3600 grams	400 grams daily
bread	2160 grams	250 grams daily
meat	230 grams	210 grams per week
margarine	120 grams	–
sugar	140 grams	–
cooking fat	60 grams	–
flour	(50) grams	18 grams
Eng tea	10 grams	–
Eng coffee	10 grams	–
jam (syrup)	175 grams	130
sauerkraut	(125) grams	–
dried peas	150 grams	)
fresh veg.	(600) grams	) 175
turnips	1800 (or 2400)	)
barley	100 (50)	)
cheese	(62.5) grams	(50)
dried veg.	(30) grams	20

(Figures in brackets are not always an issue).

Paddy and I lost by 500 points at bridge in evening. ARA stopped play when we were winning next rubber. Planes overhead.

19 February. Heating not on all day – pressure insufficient to reach here (G. excuses). Very damp, raw and cold day. Stayed in bed all morning and afternoon, and read. No parcel issue (run out)!! Potatoes and turnips for dinner, and barley for lunch!! Very 'fed up'. 'Yellow' in afternoon – distant bombing. ARA in evening. Planes overhead and heavy AA over Brunswick (bombed). Paddy and I lost by 600 points at bridge in evening. ARA late at night (planes heard).

20 February. Drizzled during day. No heating till 4.00 pm. Consequently everyone cold and miserable. It used to be on from 8.00 till 12.00 and 3.00 till 8.00 (or the ARA), and made all the difference to our comfort etc. The present German ration of food is 1,200 calories daily. Smoked my last cigarette from the ounce of tobacco I got on Sunday week!! Stayed in bed until the afternoon tea, but got up to brew tea and make toast for lunch (and spuds from mess). Read John Macmurray's *A Challenge to the Churches – Religion and Democracy*.

112

Very interesting. Blackie and I went to lecture on Russia by Britnov (a Russian captured at Arnhem) – very good, but latter half controversial, disjointed and full of platitudes – packed room. Paddy and I won by 800 points at bridge in evening, before 2 ARAs stopped play – heavy AA over Brunswick and planes passed over for a long time. ARA late at night again.

☆ ☆ ☆

22 February. No heating all day (pump not mended yet!) Turnips for lunch!! Read in bed till 2.30. ARA in morning and in afternoon (the greater part of day). Sunny day. Distant bombing during afternoon and then some 'not so distant' (!!) created a 'flap' in our room!! Went to shelter for few minutes. Markers in Hanover direction, but must have been nearer. Tony and I lost by 1,900 points to C.B. and Dicky Laws in afternoon. Very cold, very hungry, no cigarettes and very browned off!! Wrote L/C (No 105) home. German stew for dinner (after roll call). Had L/C (d. 11 November) from Uncle Charlie. ARA at night. Paddy and I winning at bridge when lights went out. Heard that Ian Thompson had escaped from an OR's camp and reached home.

23 February. Stayed in bed till the afternoon, when the water eventually came on. ARA all morning. Dull and misty day. No heating on till about 5.00 pm. Read most of day. Barley (with dried fruit from rest of parcels in it) for lunch, and potatoes for dinner. Went to Lt Col Booth's lecture after tea 'Two Years in the Philippines' (in US Army). Quite interesting. Arnhem bloke had bad luck, when he failed to walk out of gate with a lavatory seat on his shoulders. Last night, four officers arrived from Lamsdorf in Silesia after being 'loose' for a bit – apparently many were shot when trying to escape, and the rest got shot up in the train by 'typhoons', and had to walk a long way. Two days ago, the private tobacco store was broken into and 100s more cigs were stolen. Also meat has been stolen from the cookhouse. Made toast to have with the dinner potatoes. Started bridge, but ARA interfered as usual!! Planes overhead.

24 February. 2 counts on roll call. Read in bed till afternoon teatime. Got up to brew and make toast for lunch.

Potatoes from mess for lunch and dinner. Also had beetroot (from canteen) for dinner, plus toast. Heating not on till late afternoon, and even then it did not properly heat our end of building. ARA all morning – heavy formations above low clouds. Several 'Yellows' in afternoon. Paddy and I beat Tony and Jock by 4,500 points at bridge after tea. Went to bed after dinner and read a bit. No ARA till after 'lights out' when planes and AA heard.

25 February. 4 'Yellows' in morning and afternoon. Got up early in order to go to 10.00 Communion but one officer was missing on roll call, and the Goons ordered an identity check despite the SBOs giving them the name of the escapee. Eventually we were turfed out of the buildings, and were then checked up into the attics. Very cold windy day. 'Bashed' all my sugar and a lot of margarine ration in morning!! Lunch late ('pea soup' but mostly dried cabbage) due to roll call lasting so long. A German Foreign Office official was here, and was dressed in Luftwaffe uniform. Read till afternoon tea. Walked on concrete for hour with Ray C!! Then read a new edition of 'The Spectator. Heating on for a while before roll call. Made a cigarette out of some tobacco dust from my overcoat pocket!! Paddy and I won by 2,800 points at bridge in evening. ARA – planes overhead.

27 February. Stayed in bed till after tea. ARAs in morning and afternoon. Finished reading Bishop Burnet's History of his own times – very interesting, but hard-going due to bad sequence and old style of English used. Went to John Talbot's lecture after tea. Only just squeezed in! He was the Naval War Correspondent (Home Fleet) for a year in 1941-2 (Reuter's) and went on Murmansk and Archangel convoys, Vaagro and Spitzbergen raids, Atlantic Charter etc. Very interesting talk indeed lasting 1 hours. Barley soup for lunch, and 'Spam pie' for dinner – latter tasty and 'quite' filling despite minute amount of meat in it. Paddy and I lost by 1,100 points at bridge in evening. ARA and planes over. Another ARA late at night, and many more planes over.

2 March. Very windy and cold day. Snow fell at times. A pine tree blew on to house 5 last night, and 2 patches of our roof stripped of tiles. Read in bed in morning and dozed in early afternoon. Barley stew for lunch. Tony and I lost by 400 points to C.B. and Dicky Laws in afternoon in C.B.'s room. Heating on for short time in morning and afternoon, as it was not on at all yesterday. Long ARA in morning and planes over. Several 'yellows' during day. M and V stew from mess in evening – very tasty, but a bit watery!! Paddy and I 1,700 points down at bridge in evening. 2 ARAs and planes over. Things going well on Western front – Goons admit Neuss entered. 'Yellow' at night.

3 March. Was room 'stooge'. Sprinkling of snow on the ground in morning. Windy and cold, but bright and sunny day – hope visibility is as good in west!! Read in bed for half the morning, and then ARA. Dozens of formations of bombers passed over slightly to the west from the north. Very clear sky. Markers and bombs dropped south of Brunswick, on Brunswick, to the east of here and in Hanover direction. AA opened up. Went to shelter for a minute or two when I thought they were aiming for the Niemo factory, as planes were directly overhead!! However, I was wrong, thank goodness!! This last lot was the nearest dropped, and strangely enough was the only lot of bombs clearly heard. The wind must have carried the noise away. Water 'off' most of day, so I collected 3 jugfuls from tap in hospital basement. Brewed hot water for shaving. Turnip soup for lunch. Divided sugar and marg ration in afternoon, also read a bit. Heating on for periods in morning and afternoon, but pressure not as good as before the fuel rationing came in. Wrote P.C. (No 107) home. Paddy and I won by 1,000 points at bridge in afternoon. Shower baths after roll call at 5.45 pm in House 1 – they were originally at 2.20, but there was no water then. Water off most of evening as well. Several 'yellows' in afternoon. Fish-pie from mess in evening. Very good. Also mint tea, as we have now run out of all Red X brews. Started bridge in evening, but ARA and planes over. Another ARA and several 'yellows' during the night.

4 March. Roll call at 9.00 (inside) after 12 hours in bed!! Snow on ground and snowing hard, but changed to rain later on. Water 'on and off' all day. Started using the steam cookhouse again, but very unsatisfactory due to bad pressure (I think). Ersatz coffee nearly an hour late for breakfast; lunch ('sauerkraut soup') over an hour late; no afternoon 'mint tea' at all; and dinner which should have been at 4.30 could not be served till after roll call. Went to Choral Eucharist at 10.00. Read the 'British Industries' section of the 'Good Living' exhibition before lunch. Read a bit in afternoon, and then visited Andy and Blackie. Heating on for short time in morning and afternoon, but very cold day. German stew for dinner and mint tea – neither very hot, but nevertheless welcome! Paddy and I lost by 7,000 points at bridge in evening!! Dreadful cards, and very dull. No ARAs at all during day. 2 ARAs and several 'yellows' during the night – planes over and distant bombing. News that German coal ration bombed on way, and so we have a further cut in mess rations and no heating except at weekends! Froze at night.

5 March. Heating 'just' on for short time in morning. Read in bed in morning. Several warnings including 2 'reds' – planes over. Nothing from the mess for lunch. Brewed tea, and had bread and marg. Went to Ackroyd's lecture on Parliamentary History from the American War of Independence to the Parliamentary Reform Bill of 1832. Mint tea at 3.00. Went to debate in afternoon – Solomons proposed that 'Economic and Social Equality be the dominant aim in 20th Century Britain'. The opposer was very weak and lost by about 120 to 30 votes. Water 'on and off' all day. Rainy day. Started reading *Jamaica Inn* by Daphne du Maurier. News that some other camps on *full* parcels!! 'Boiled potatoes' for dinner and no hot water. Brewed tea and made toast after roll call. My 'spuds' were cold when I came up, so I heated them up and also re-heated tea and toast!! Paddy and I were winning by 1,000 points at bridge in evening when ARA stopped play. Planes, AA and flare over Brunswick. (This morning and from now onwards roll call is at 9.00 and 9.30 on Sundays.)

6 March. Never sleep continuously at night nowadays, as we usually get to bed about 7.30 to 8.30 and have 12 or more hours in bed!! Since short rations, I have started to dream at night (which I never did before)! Went to lavatory for first time for 3 days!! (Nothing 'to move'!!) No alarms during the day. 'Pots' for lunch and pea soup for dinner. ARA at night.

7 March. Read in bed in morning and early afternoon.

Cold day. No heating at all now, as usual. Sauerkraut soup for lunch (very thin, and where were pots?). Went to 'Crazy Gang' after tea – very enjoyable, and quite good under the circumstances. Turnip soup for dinner. ARA and 'yellow' in afternoon. Read in bed till ARA – very heavy formations and planes overhead, continued Ack Ack and distant bombing (very heavy) – roar of planes 'for hours'. 'Yellow' later on in night.

8 March. Finished reading *Jamaica Inn*. Very good book. Snowing in morning, but it turned to drizzle. Cold day. Water 'on and off'. Went to Ackroyd's lecture on the Problem of the Electorate and Ballots in democracy. Got Daphne du Maurier's *Frenchman's Creek* out of library. News that International Red X had come to agreement with Germans to send Red X parcels by road – hope some soon turn up!! 'Goons' treacle issue. Potatoes for lunch, and German stew for dinner. Made toast. 'Yellow' alarm in afternoon. Paddy and I winning by 2,100 points at bridge in evening. ARA – fell asleep early and woke up during 'yellow' when planes and AA heard – distant bombing?

11 March. Dull day, but very little wind for a change. Roll call at 9.30. Was going to Sung Eucharist, but did not realize time till too late. Chopped a bit of wood. Pots for lunch and German stew for dinner. Brewed tea for both meals (as Bert was Room stooge) and made toast for a lunch. We also 'bashed' our dinner's bread at lunchtime, as we only got 3 very small and bad potatoes. Read latest edition of 'Spectator' after lunch. Finished reading *Frenchman's Creek* – enjoyed it very much after all, especially the descriptions of the countryside etc. in the spring and hot weather, but I wish food was not mentioned so often!! Went to Matins at 4.00 pm, after getting *Lord Jim* by Joseph Conrad out of library. 'Yellow' and ARA in afternoon – distant bombing and planes overhead. Heating on for short time in evening. Went to bed early – ARA and planes over.

12 March. Pots and (!!) 'Swill Soup' for lunch – latter would not bear investigation and smelt foul, but certainly was welcome and quite greasy!! (bone been boiled in it!!) Dried veg soup for dinner (mostly sauerkraut and therefore very bitter). Wrote L/C (No 109) home. We are all finding that we are eating a tremendous amount of salt since we have been on short rations, also 'visits' to the lavatory are very scarce!! Nowadays we always get to bed before the ARA (roughly 7.45 to 8.00) as the lights never come on again and anyway it is too cold, so we get thirteen or so hours in bed although not asleep all the time.

☆ ☆ ☆

14 March. Twins' birthday. Read in bed till after lunch (potatoes). Cheese and cooking fat issue. Sunny day and quite warmish, almost spring-like. Strolled about outside most of afternoon. 2 ARAs in afternoon – very heavy and continuous bombing in Hanover direction. Went to library and got *Sir Richard Grenville of the 'Revenge'* by A.L. Rowse out. Parcel rumour pretty strong but incorrect!! Turnip soup for dinner. Felt quite tired after my 'outing' today!!

15 March. Finished reading *Lord Jim* – very drawn-out book. Got up for lunch (potatoes). 'Bashed' treacle ration!! Lovely day, and quite warm in the sun. Buds beginning to show green. Sat in sun till teatime (mint tea as usual). ARA all afternoon – saw fighters pass over; heard lots of planes to the north, but could not see due to the haze. Heard bombing, and AA to the south. Walked round for an hour with Andy in 'the Wood' after tea. Tomorrow or the next day, the SMO is going to a meeting of SMOs at Berlin. What for?? Missed Ackroyd's lecture on the merits etc. of the multi- and single-party systems – I was going to the lecture when the ARA sounded, and then presumed it would not be held, but unfortunately it was. German stew for dinner (flavour of onions, but mostly turnip). 'Bull' and 'Flash' brought gramophone in our room in evening. ARA and planes heard – very heavy raid in Hanover direction, and the camp buildings shook. Flashes etc. to the NW.

☆ ☆ ☆

17 March. Indoor roll call – raining. Stayed in bed most of day. Brewed up and made toast for lunch and dinner. Potatoes for lunch and barley soup for dinner. Bert and I 'bashed' tomorrow's bread as well. Jim and I put new bed up in room (to exchange for ours), but the bed boards were too long!! News that 383 new officers (including 65 ORs) are *definitely* coming from Hadamer (or Linburg) senior officers' camp, and that the German HQ is moving with them. They are due tomorrow and we hope they bring parcels with them!! Paddy and I 1,000 points up at bridge in evening. ARA and a few planes over. During the night, a single plane made four 'run-ins' after dropping a flare, dropped a bomb, and made fifth trip to see the result. I was asleep and vaguely heard the bang, but it was in direction of bridge and canal. There was also some machine-gunning (autobahn?).

19 March. Coffee at 8.15, and identity check at 9.00, lasting nearly till 11.00 (ie. hospital took so long). Talked to Wilf on gardening. Strolled round before lunch (potatoes, stockpot soup and tomorrow's bread ration!!). Sunny day but not very warm. 25 cigs issued yesterday, and I swapped them for '3 Castles' cig. tobacco (1 ounce – mild – too mild!!). Went to Ackroyd's lecture on 'Rise and Fall of Parliamentary Government' from 3rd Reform Bill (1864?) till the last war with special reference to the transference of power from the Commons and Lords to the cabinet as a result of single-member constituencies, plurality (not majority) and the party system. Two 'yellows' in afternoon, and distant bombing (?) to the W.S.W. Laundry started up at a reduced rate (1,000 pants, 1,000 shirts, 1,000 socks for whole camp). I sent pair of u/ pants. Jim and I sawed ends off new bed-boards (too long) before tea (ordinary tea, ie. not mint tea). Some companies (4?) issued with parcels. After tea, we put the new bed up in room and shifted our kit to it. We also moved cupboards etc. and had a partial 'spring clean'. Quite exhausting!! News that two trucks of Canadian parcels were sent off on 14 March. The truck which came yesterday had been dive-bombed, machine-gunned and pilfered; and 120 parcels were missing. However, we still have just over enough for a half issue. Two extra cigs issued today. News that Paddy Webb, Robbie Mason and Greenwood have arrived safely at a Marlag in North Germany. The Mess is taking all meats, fish, puddings etc. out of parcels in order to spread it out over a fortnight or so (pending arrival of more parcels). My cold has been pretty miserable today. Mixed veg soup for dinner. Ate the other half of tomorrow's bread!! Paddy and I 1,700 points up at bridge in evening. 'Yellow' at night. (For the last week or two, the water situation has been normal.) Saw in the *Spectator* that Bill Bowes has provisionally accepted the Wardenship of the Brunswick Boys' Club, as he thinks that probably his cricketing days are over. He says that the normal 'life' of a fast bowler is only 10 years, and he has had 10 years besides the war. He expects to be with Yorkshire till the end of 1946 in order to see what plans (if any) they have for him, before accepting the wardenship definitely.

23 March. Short ARA after roll call. Was room 'stooge'. Another ARA later on and one in afternoon. Distant bombing (?) heard all three times to the west and south. Lovely warm and sunny day. Sat outside in morning, and had hair cut outside. Oatmeal porridge (very good) from mess for lunch. Had cocoa. (1/3 tin cocoa and eggs issued yesterday.) Tommy Sampson's band played in the open air from 2 till 2.45 at the south end of the 'wood'. Very enjoyable, and quite hot lying in the sun. Went to Capt Baker's lecture on 'The English Political Scene' from a Tory Reform point of view. Very good. Pea soup from Mess for dinner, and Bert gave me a few spuds. Paddy and I 3,600 points down at bridge in evening – Paddy played shockingly badly!! ARA in evening and planes over.

24 March. Sunny and warm day, but coldish breeze. Sat outside for a bit in morning. Cooked spuds for Bert and he gave me his lunchtime ration, so we fried spuds and had scrambled eggs on toast for lunch. Very good! Letter card dated Boxing Day from Mum – news that my letters of 13th and 26th October got home, the latter on Xmas Eve; 'orchard is not quite what we expected . . . head gardeners somewhat misled us and so one feels disappointed . . . plum tree blooming out of season!!' 'Plenty of parcels reported on way to all camps'!! Shaved and had 'wash-bath' in afternoon. Went to Capt Astbury's lecture on the English political scene from the 'Left' point of view. Very good talk. Brewed water for cocoa and made toast for dinner. 'Salmon kedgeree' from Mess (very good 'soup-like' pottage). Paddy and I 1,700 points up at bridge in evening. ARA and planes over. Several 'yellows' and distant bombing during the day. Bert made cocoa in the evening.

25 March. Brazilian coffee for breakfast. Lovely warm and sunny day. Sewed my BD trousers up. Put screws into bottom of my stool. ARA in morning, and many markers some distance to the NE, but could not hear bombing. Went to Matins. Made toast for dinner (potatoes and cocoa). Wrote L/C (No 112) home). Yesterday's German communique admitted crossings of Rhine between Rees and Wesel in the north. The leaves on the small trees coming out well. Washed boots, and polished them and my shoes! Listened to Tommy Sampson's band before tea outside houses 6 and 7. Read *Spectator* in afternoon, and visited Blackie who had a bad foot. Brewed cocoa for the evening meal. German stew (quite good) from Mess. Paddy and I 1,000 points up at bridge in evening. Usual ARA and planes over.

26 March. Sat outside in sunshine. It was warm, but the wind got up and I went in. Weather turned cloudy and cold in afternoon. Read a bit in morning. Very good 'Bacon and Sausage Pie' from Mess for lunch, and Bert Ash gave me a few chips. Had cocoa. We also ate most of today's bread ration, the balance we 'bashed' for tea!! Went to a lecture in Ackroyd's series on 'The Rise and Fall of Parliamentary Government' in afternoon. He dealt with the delegation of unlimited powers from PC to the Ministries, the growth of Administrative Law (without Courts) resulting from this, and the formation of the Inner War Cabinet and Imperial War Cabinets during and after the last war. Handed a shirt in for laundry in morning. The camp received an Xmas card (photo of Royal Family) from the King and Queen. Two noticeable features of undernourishment: (1) how tiring it is to carry greatcoat on one arm and (2) how boney one's BTM and thighs are when sitting on stool or lying in bed!! Went to debate on the future of the BBC's Charter in afternoon. The House voted (99 v 38) for the renewal of its Charter. Tony Maxtone-Graham proposed that it should be discontinued, and that commercial advertising be instituted. Jim and I did not vote – undecided!! Very good debate. Brewed cocoa for dinner. Quite good 'dried veg soup' from Mess. Wrote P.C. (No 113) to Daddy. 'Yellow' alarm (or 2?) during day. Paddy and I 700 points up at bridge in evening. Usual ARA.

☆ ☆ ☆

28 March. Brazilian coffee for breakfast. Read in bed in morning. ARA planes over and distant AA all morning. Dull cloudy day. Did a little toast and brewed some extra coffee for lunch (Pots). (Yesterday, Dicky Laws had letter from home saying that POWs are going to Rehabilitation Camps for a month before our leave on our return home. Don't like the idea!!) Finished reading *Sir R Grenville* – dull book. Got *Silver Ley* by Adrian Bell out of the library. Tony Jacobs and I drew with Dicky Laws and Keith Sisterton at bridge in afternoon. Pea soup for dinner. Paddy and I 200 points down at bridge in evening. No ARA at all during night.

29 March. Rumour that a 'road-transport' truck of parcels had arrived. Everyone's 'local morale' up, and then we heard that it was a YMCA lorry with toilet paper etc!!

☆ ☆ ☆

31 March. ARA during roll call. Very heavy formations of planes over after we were dismissed. Bombing in direction of the town, the autobahn and bridges, and the aerodrome. Some bombs too near to be pleasant, so went to shelter for some time. The whine of some bombs heard. Read in bed in morning and afternoon. Water off most of day (after raid). Brewed cocoa and made toast for lunch (pots). Bert made toast for tea (milk in brew from Mess). Had 'wash-bath' and shaved and polished boots before roll call. Barley and veg soup for dinner. Had more bread, and have eaten 2 days' ration today!! Cold dull day. Electricity off till about 5.00 pm, and then very poor light. Paddy and I 1,200 down at bridge in evening. 2 'yellows' at night – one or two explosions and machine-gunning in the distance on autobahn (?). Pants back from laundry.

2 April. EASTER MONDAY. Dull day. Rained hard after tea. Tea for breakfast, pots and stock pot soup for lunch; milk with tea at 2.45, and barley and veg soup for dinner. Read in bed in morning and early afternoon. Sent a shirt to laundry. Wrote L/ C (No 114) home. Read the latest number of the *Spectator*. Noticed how far out the trees are now. Brewed extra tea for dinner. The Commandant says he no longer expects the new arrivals from Hamadar!! We seem to be a very lucky camp, considering the stories we hear of camps being evacuated from the east on foot with scant rations etc, resulting in ill health and death. Went to *French Without Tears* in Annex in evening. Good effort considering the rations and other difficulties. The German Foreign Office Official was there. No ARAs during the day, but two at night. Very many planes overhead especially during the second alarm. One odd bomb and a bit of M.G. fire from single aircraft (in direction of autobahn?).

3 April. Rained most of day. Read in bed in morning. Pots for lunch, and Bert gave me cocoa. Went to sleep till after tea (with milk) – feeling very 'browned off', hungry etc. and not even inclined to read. Went to talk on 'Some Aspects of Post-War USA' by Col Hoban of US Army – dealing especially with Social Credit, and very interesting. Fish kedgeree (sort of barley-potato-and fish soup) for dinner. Brewed some coffee (which Bert had) for evening meal. Finished bread off (should have lasted till Friday!!) Everyone 'down in the dumps'!! Why don't those Goons give in?!! Nothing special in evening. 2 ARAs and 'yellow' during night. Very many planes over during second alarm; but there was a lot of activity the whole time. 2 lots of machine-gunning, one burst following a flare quite close in the west.

☆ ☆ ☆

5 April. Dull day. Several 'yellow' alarms. Stayed in bed till teatime. Oatmeal-cum-barley porridge for lunch. Ate treacle issue and some of today's bread. Read a bit. American parcel issue between 6. 2 meats, fish and raisins went into Mess. We got 15 cigs, 2 biscuits and 2 ascorbic acid tablets, 2 big squares of chocolate, tiny portion of very good peach jam, portions of cheddar cheese, very good peanut butter, ordinary butter, powdered milk and lump sugar. Had very good afternoon tea including more bread, and felt satisfied for a change. In fact, after my first cigarette for some time, I felt a little sick for a short time!! Strolled around the camp. News that another 2,000 Canadian parcels dispatched from Lubeck on 13 March and another (different) 2,000 have been diverted here. That means that 8,000 are now 'on the way' by rail!! Unconfirmed report that one stuck at Brunswick Station (!!??). German stew for dinner. Brewed American coffee for our syndicate of four. Had milk and sugar in it. Also had a piece of toast and cheese. plus chocolate. Felt *very* full . . . nearly as bad as Xmas Day!! Morale up in evening!! Paddy and I 4,000 points down at bridge in evening. Dreadful cards again. 'Yellow' alarm in evening. Quite enlightened conversation (for a change!!) in room after lights went out – re-cycling in England and motor cycles etc. Some Protected Personnel saw two slogans written on a bridge during their walk: vis. 'Hail! Amerikaner!' and 'Down With Hitler'. No one in the camp seemed to sleep during night (excitement).

6 April. Rained most of day. ARA in morning. Finished reading *Military Memoirs* – quite interesting in parts. Stayed in bed till tea. Excellent lunch from Mess – cold meat rolls (1/5 tin), pickled veg, (beetroot and tinned veg) and lashed potatoes. Bert brewed American coffee. News that 4,000 more Canadian parcels left Goteburg (by rail) on 19 March – 12,000 now 'on the way' and overdue!! Rumour of one track at station is still current but not official!! (Supposed to be not addressed to this camp.) Got *Garden Rubbish and Other Country Bumps* by W.C. Sellar and R.J. Yeatman out of library. Visited Andy in afternoon. A small dried fruit issue in afternoon. Heated this up to add to a very poor barley-porridge from Mess for dinner. Also brewed American coffee. Paddy and I 1,600 points up at bridge in evening. 'Goons' admit we have reached Hamelin, 50 miles slightly south of west of Brunswick. 'Yellow' in evening. A lot of Goon air activity – aerodrome being evacuated? Also a lot of activity on the roads (including tracked vehicles).

☆　☆　☆

8 April. Turned out sunny in the end, but very cold wind. Went to Sung Eucharist. ARA all morning and 'yellow' in afternoon. Distant bombing. A bit of a 'flap' in afternoon when a high-flying fighter cleared its guns and a sentry fired an odd shot!! Toad-in-the-hole, gravy and potatoes for lunch – very tasty, but as usual very little!! Read *The Spectator*. Strolled around most of the day (with Blackie before tea). Usual rumours prevalent. Finished making guide to SW England out for Wilf in afternoon. German stew for dinner. Darned 2 pairs of socks in evening. No truth in rumour that ORs had moved from Fallingsbostal!! 2 ARAs in evening (early), and 6 medium bombers bombed objectives in Brunswick area. Missed the fun (indoors). ARA at night, and distant gunfire (??). Brewed tea in evening. Morale up!

9 April. Sunny day, but still a cold wind. Read in bed in morning. Brewed tea leaves again for lunch (potatoes). Bread issue (½ loaf for 3 days), and ate most of it during the day as it was hot and new!! 'Mooched' about most of day – everyone waiting and rather impatient!! Chatted with Andy. ARAs including 'short ones' all day long. A lot of blasting going on. Last week's laundry (1 shirt) came back dirty. The previous week's has not returned. Letter dated 20 November from Aline. News that 2,000 Canadian parcels at Brunswick station, definitely, and they will be at Querum tomorrow morning. Later on, 1,000 American parcels arrived by road (destined for Hildersheim but latter 'cut off'). Today is my day in our room 'Armistice Sweepstake' but no Yanks turned up yet!! Collected brushwood before roll call, and Bert and I got 'wood' in evening!! 3 American cigs issued in evening. Potato ration cut by 120 grams a day and turnip ration increased!! M and V stew for dinner (the last of the Karlsruhr truck which arrived a few weeks ago). Goon communique admitted fall of Hildesheim. ARA at night, and planes over. Got list of London restaurants for foreign foods from Sam.

10 April. Did not wake up in early hours of the morning when a lot of 'shooting' went on in the Brunswick direction. Heavy gunfire in direction of town when daylight came and it seemed to move round to the SE during the morning. Misty on roll call but turned out a lovely warm and sunny day with very little wind. Another half of loaf issued (to last up to Saturday). Letter dated 4 December from Mum. Read in bed for some of morning. Potatoes (neat!!) for lunch. Sat outside afterwards, till our company had parcel issue (unpunctured) – American parcel between three (1 tin M and V to Mess) and 30 cigs after tea. Had a good afternoon tea!! News that the railway truck is 'temporarily lost'!! ARAs all day long – a lot of fighters machine-gunned the rear aerodrome and districts all round us; the other 2 aerodromes bombed all in morning; 100s (or 1000s) of bombers passed to the north going eastwards in afternoon; many fighters 'stooging' around and the rocket-firing ones dived over Brunswick (or S of it) in early evening. Practically all the garrison except the most decrepit left the camp (for Brunswick), but the Commandant and Hertzog (Foreign Office Rep), (both good chaps), remained behind. Rumours that the town is surrounded, that white flags flying from windows, that Union Jacks in troops' pockets. Demolitions going on all day – a big fire due west, lots of oil 'went up' on this aerodrome, and the 2 big railway bridges over the canal to the NW went in the evening. More gunfire from Brunswick direction in late afternoon! News that 'no chance' of a move now – feel greatly relieved, but had been convinced of this all today. Still quite a lot of Luftwaffe about. Strolled about after tea, with Bert Steel for a while. Everyone just 'waiting' but much more contentedly than yesterday (full stomach and confidence!!), although no one can concentrate on reading due to excitement. More fighters circling round in evening. Very good pea soup with meat in it for dinner. Also had a snack as I had got 1/8th of loaf for cigs. (Bert and I not touching today's loaf till day after tomorrow!!) Had good brew of coffee after dinner. Feeling very satisfied, though not 'full'!! Just missed a 'dog fight' while writing this diary up. Signed for the *Victory Spectator* to be sent to me after the war (Returned POW Association). A few day's ago I signed for *Artist's Proof* to be sent to me. Gunfire getting *very* close (at dusk). MG fire from near aerodrome (??). Brewed coffee in evening. Constant and very loud demolitions going all round at night especially to the NW and N. ARA and single planes 'stooging' about. Artillery increased and became louder throughout the night – spasmodic at first. Counter-battery fire. One Goon gun seemed to be quite near, but believe the nearest of our shells landed about a mile away (although they seemed *much* too close!!). Impossible to sleep as the noise was terrific. Over half the room went down to shelter to sleep. I gave up trying to sleep before 3.30, and took my bedding down to shelter. Slept for one or two hours, as the noise was deadened down there. The artillery increased to a very heavy barrage at 5.30 am, and general belief that the attack went in then (?) – ie. tomorrow.

11 April. Water off. Got up as barrage was dying down, and had a wash in my bowl. Moved bedding upstairs. Brew of coffee (very welcome!) and a good snack – including a 'bash' of Nestles' powdered milk!! Everyone smoking very heavily!! Pall of smoke hanging over Brunswick and the country to the west. I was room 'stooge'. More oil burning on aerodrome. Machine-gun fire and spasmodic gunfire to the south and in direction of Brunswick. Strolled round a bit and had a 'rear' in outside latrine!! Beautiful warm and sunny day. Last of Luftwaffe girls left by truck. Made a brew of coffee and had a 'snack' at 11.30!! Where 'the hell' are our troops and what are they doing?!! Many fighters about in morning, and dozens of them poured rockets into Brunswick and also dropped an odd bomb. Suppose this means our troops cannot be there!! The remainder of the mail came into camp. Mail Department now closed down!! I had 2 letters from Mum dated 10 December and New Year's Day. News that M had another letter from Graham Boyton with details of the hand-cuffing which she already knew about from the authorities. Also that Aunt Dora had died (nearly 80); Raymond Stephen was killed by lightning in July at Luft VI. Next Saturday's margarine issue came in. No roll call in morning!! Lunch late (at 1.00) – tasty spam pie but small portion of course. More fighters over before lunch. Weather clouded over slightly. Can distinctly hear the whine of the shells to the south. Copied Ham's recipe for Halwa into my Log Book. Sat in the hot sun during afternoon. Dozens of Thunderbolts attacked Brunswick (or S of it?) with rockets, machine-gun fire and bombs – diving down one after the other. Spasmodic gunfire continued in direction of town, and to the south. Electricity off all day, but no worries!! News that enough Goon rations till Sunday week are 'outside the wire', but that no hope of parcel truck (looting). Water ran out even in reserve taps inside the camp in evening. Fish 'kedgeree' for dinner. Bert and I had some of tomorrow's bread!! Brewed coffee and made slice of fried bread each outside. Had small 'bash' of 'Klim', and only marge left out of 1/3rd of a parcel now (besides meats)!! Roll call inside in evening. Water is being got from outside pond to the Mess for breakfast brews – has to be boiled for hour (typhoid). Bed early (no lights), and had a wonderful night's sleep. Very little gunfire.

The Yanks arrive!

12 April. *'Der tag!'* The Yanks arrived at 9.15!! I was in bed, but rushed out in time in pyjamas and greatcoat. Terrific cheer as 'jeeps' arrived – a patrol of the 125th Cavalry Recce Squadron of the 5th Cavalry attached to the 30th US Infantry Division: (9th US Army). Got autographs of two of them. Capt A. Plower (i/c) reported L of C clear. They had learnt of the camp only from someone on the road, while following up Panzers to the east. Volksturm reported to have been a nuisance with Panzerfaust, but otherwise very little opposition though minor hold-ups due to demolitions on the road.

They later went down to contact troops in Brunswick which is almost clear. Made 2 big slices of fried bread and fried American sausage meat for Bert and me for breakfast!! Also brewed coffee. Very satisfied!! Sugar issue in morning. Watched activity at gate. US troops threw some rations in, but was not successful in scramble. French and Ukranian POWs and workers gathering round the wire. Union Jack on gate. Jack Tonge brought big civilian wireless set in – he had done great job on 'canary' (our wireless set) which was operating even yesterday when no power on. Letters d 17 December from Mum and 20 December from Drake. 2 more barrel-fuls and 4 sackfuls have come in since and are being sorted!! Our own camp police 'on' at the gate, and cameras 'brought' out!! Toast, potatoes, and good cup of coffee for lunch – not thinking about food much now!! Treacle issue. Official news that 9th US had reached the Elbe near Madgelung after a lightning advance, having overcome stiff opposition at 'Hermann Goering' works south of Brunswick. L/C d 19 November and P.C. dated 24 November from Mum. The Goons were rounded up very easily this morning, quite resigned to their fate. Paddy Wilson won the Room Armistice Sweepstake today (£1 each). Cleaned my boots and shoes!! Had a good wash, shave etc. as soon as water came on in afternoon. British, Canadian and US War Correspondents here. The American took messages from a few US POWs to record to America on Sunday. Armoured cars etc. arrived later on. An odd bit of gunfire in morning, but died down later on. Overcast day with spots of rain, but 'nothing can mar our joy'!! Tore up a lot of old letters for 'toast fuel'. SBO's parade at 3.30. 'Thanksgiving Service' at 4.15 on parade ground, loaf of bread issued afterwards. Many of our officers outside the camp fixing up supplies, utility services etc. Lights came on in evening. News that Maj Gen Veith twice refused Col Dandridge's (GI of US 30th Infantry Division) ultimatum to surrender the town, but that resistance was slight and very few American casualties. Dandridge had breakfast with Veith and former believes that latter's decision was influenced by his SS ADC. Col Strehle (ex-commandant) was taken prisoner wounded. Brunswick not recognized as open city due to refusal of surrender. The town was cleared last night by the 30th Div which had come from Hamelin. Very good thick

German stew for dinner. Brewed coffee. News from Q.M. that 'bags' of looted food being brought to the cookhouse!! The American 9th Army have taken so many prisoners in this push that they say it might be several days before we are moved back and that we shall probably go direct to England. News from Intelligence Offr of 30th Division that (i) Magdeburg fell yesterday afternoon, and bridge over Elbe captured intact; (ii) barely 12 American casualties in Brunswick, and over 3,000 prisoners; (iii) a British colonel taken over Brunswick, but foreign workers completely out of control; Germans quiet and praying for arrival of occupation troops. News over radio that 'very little known' about situation round Brunswick but that 'fierce resistance' being met!!! A wireless was fixed up with loudspeaker from first floor of hospital in evening, but only foreign music coming over. Got a large handful of dehydrated meat (Goon) from one of the Yankee trucks in the camp. Bert

Our Liberators

and I had supper at 8.00!! – tea, and scrambled eggs (dried) on toast. One of the US troops said that the artillery had a big barrage organized for this morning on the aerodrome including these buildings – as they did not know this camp was here!! Listened to the BBC news at 9.00 pm outside – news that Brunswick by-passed to the N and S; the town entered; and fighting in the centre!! Bernie Kendrick gave our room some custard. Could not sleep for a long time at night – due to excitement, and the heat (the latter as a result of a full tummy, which was certainly 'working overtime'). 'Terror-fliegers' on their usual trip to Berlin at night, but hold no terror for us now!!

13 April. Power off, so could not hear the 9.00 news. The Americans say that Roosevelt has just died. Barley porridge from Mess for breakfast. Made some toast, and had some 'K' ration cheese with it which Bert had procured. Listened to 10.00 European Service News. Wrote L/C home. Sunny day at times, but cloudy most of time. 1/5 tin of tinned German liver sausage and potatoes for lunch. Brewed tea and put sausage meat on fried bread. News that we are probably moving today. US 'C' ration issued (no cigs in our room's box). Wilf and Jim got pass out of camp; and made souvenirs of German Air Force caps, dress bayonets etc. Started sorting kit out in afternoon. Very unpleasant outside, as the wind was blowing all the burning rubbish about. Bert had indigestion in afternoon!! Had half a raw onion, 1/4 'K' ration cheese (issued) and toast for tea. Cooking fat and loaf issued per person as well. Dinner very late at 6.45, but we had a brew of tea, some toast and curdled creamed rice (from Bernie) at 6.00. The Mess later put on a very good M and V stew. Ate one tin of 'C' ration biscuits (supposed to be for travelling). Collected books from library to take on journey. Water 'on and off' all day, and electricity mostly off. News that a British colonel, a POW Contact Officer attached to 9th American Army, said he thought the Americans were over-optimistic about moving us; he thinks at least a few days and probably more. He also said we would get a month's leave with 2 months' rations. Both these statements have made everyone impatient!! – but we are still 'standing-to'. 300 of the ORs in Brunswick were moved to just outside the camp from the worst of their quarters in the town. Several of our officers went down to Brunswick to act as interpreters for the authorities. 9.00 pm news said that still 'fighting in Brunswick'. German planes dropped a few bombs and machine-gunned the town at night!

14 April. I was Coy Ord Offr. Went round rooms with the time at 8.00 am. Then brewed tea and made fried bread with dehydrated meat and chopped onion on it. Barley porridge from Mess at 9.00. (10.00 am European Service news said that Brunswick 'finally cleared'!!) Dull morning, but warm and sunny afternoon. Nothing special in morning. Good mixed soup, potatoes and 1/4 (big) tin of excellent German pork (!!) for lunch. Sugar, treacle, biscuit and energy tablet issued. Bert brought some bread, sweets and cigar back from unofficial 'outing' in morning. We went out (roughly parties of 5) from 1.30 to 3.00. Wilf, Tony, Duncan, John and I went out onto aerodrome – foreign workers living in their settlements; many smashed planes lying around aerodrome; 'panzerfausts' strewn all over the place; excellent workshops abandoned. All the quarters had been thoroughly looted, but I got a piece of cheese, a German lanyard and a plate. Very enjoyable stroll and grand to be 'free' again. A message to POWs was received from Gen Eisenhower saying 'be patient' and 'expect uncomfortable journey'. Had bath in basement in afternoon – hot water!! Bert and I cooked 'Pork and Beans' ('C' ration) on 3 pieces of toast; also had a brew of tea, bread and treacle, and an excellent M and V stew (not finished) from Mess. Followed this with nearly bottle of poor red wine (issue) and cigar. Feeling too full!! Some people got Hock and some gin. Bert brought a big clock and a teddy-bear to the room in afternoon!! John and I strolled out of camp in evening. Looked at the house of flats near the outside hospital. It had been thoroughly looted of everything except the heaviest articles of furniture. The owners had obviously left in a hurry, and it's a shame to see so much good furniture and personal belongings being wasted. Did the black-out in evening. The 9.00 Home Service news announced that Oflag 79 had been overrun by the Americans!! Warmed up remainder of stew for supper. Feeling much too full!!

15 April. Dull day. Went to Communion at 8.00. Had barley porridge, pork and beans and hash and veg on toast for breakfast. Very distant bombing in morning (yesterday a

132

Goon jet-propelled plane was seen). Jock Thoms, John Williams and I walked down to the Biemode village beyond the autobahn bridge (over secondary road) to the NW. Jock eventually left us. We spoke to many German civilians, and 2 French girls. Got 2 eggs given once; got 4 more for piece of soap; got 3 sticks rhubarb given; and finally we went to a house where we met a man, his wife and two children. We got very friendly and they provided 4 eggs (gave John 3) for shaving stick. Then they gave us both a cigar and a tin of plums when we offered them a cigarette. None of the Germans seemed hostile, and most were friendly. Very few foreign workers about (thank goodness), as they had all gone into the town. Enjoyed strolling about an inhabited village very much. Tinned pork, 2 boiled eggs, potatoes and toast for lunch. Bert had been to suburbs of Brunswick and brought me back some tobacco, a cigar holder, cig roller, sugar and biscuits. Stewed the rhubarb after tea. About 2 dozen of the hospital left for Hidersheim to travel by air to England – will be in England for tea!! Helped Andy and Ripkin to fix electricity supply before dinner. Weighed myself – 57 kilograms ie. 8 stone 13–1/4 approx; an increase of kilo since 18 March, but between then and now I must have been much less. Meat and pea stew from Mess for dinner. Bert and I also had cold stewed rhubarb, tinned plums (or damsons) and a small US Army ration date pudding. Did hour camp Police duty with Duncan in evening – Bert brewed an excellent cup of coffee afterwards. News that the foreign workers all refusing to work in Brunswick, the Russians made trouble this morning; the Poles are troublesome; the Ukranians loathe the Russians; and that American tanks pouring through Brunswick. Fried eggs on toast for supper – too full!! Candlelight in evening. Indigestion at night.

16 April. Fried eggs on toast and 'chopped ham and egg' on toast plus tea for breakfast in bed at 7.30!! Barley porridge from Mess at 9.00 pm. Paddy and I walked to Brunswick. Hot and sunny day. Put collar and tie on my shirt, and cleaned my boots before setting off. Stopped on the way to the town to talk to an Irishwoman who married a German. Paddy borrowed a bicycle and went back for some tea to give her. Despite all this trouble, she would not or could not provide eggs or white bread!! Had diarrhoea and went to 'Lats' four times during morning and early afternoon (yesterday's rhubarb?)!! Brunswick itself was 'dead' – very severe bomb damage; very few people about (not even foreign workers); and 'stacks' of American transport pouring through. (Some people saw 1000s of Goon prisoners passing through on way from Elbe front.) Paddy and I met Wilf and Bert on way down. They had had lunch at an American HQ Mess; and fell in afterwards with the Dutchman (in US Army) whom we had earlier seen with motor bike. They brought back a lot of tinned food, and Bert gave me a small camera. Paddy and I very tired after long walk. Picked up some rhubarb and *one* egg on way back! Arrived back after tea and had lunch. Dinner at 6.15 pm. I shall no longer write about food (menus etc.) as we can have more or less what we like – tinned fruit, jam, wine (French Vermouth this evening) etc., etc. Milk is the commodity we mainly miss, but, having tried most things now, and still look forward to roast beef etc., fish, white bread, butter, good jam etc. However, our stomachs are working overtime, and mine especially is doing a wonderful job – touch wood!! Some people have overdone it, and are sick and in hospital. Plenty of cigars about, and 7 cigs (from American parcels left over) issued today. The Americans having trouble with Nazi snipers in Brunswick, but they 'give them the works'. A Dakota landed on Waggum aerodrome today. Lots of rumours of our moving imminently and in different ways following the visit of a Brigadier today, and the arrival of about 10 lorries this evening. Sam Sturgeon brought me an 88 mm ammo box in evening (for my kit). Check roll call in evening. Dozens of looted cars in camp looking quite like a car park!! More stories of the Russians causing a nuisance of themselves today. Fallingsbostal was in the news in evening – an American correspondent described its release and the POWs march from Poland. Wrote P.C. to be taken home by our vanguard (6 company) which leaves early tomorrow morning.

17 April. Paddy and I walked down to the Frenchman we met yesterday. He was out at first, but his comrades invited us in and gave us 2 glasses of home-brewed alcohol (Calvados) plus a bottle of undiluted to take away!! When Pol Mazuelle returned we went round several farms collecting eggs. He paid for them with marks. We got 11 eggs. Hot and sunny day. John and I set off to get some milk in afternoon, but a truck-

134

load of froggies asked us to go with them to collect provisions from a store which our ORs were guarding. The store was the one on the canal with the big cranes. Before the arrival of our ORs it had been looted by the Russians, but I got some brown sugar, some energy tablets, and a jar of gooseberries – the latter given to me by ORs. We tried unsuccessfully to get milk on the way back. Plenty of bottled fruit of every kind has been obtained by our syndicate. Roll call in evening. Brewed tea afterwards. C.B. heard from a chap in 15th Scottish Division that on our return we go to a reception camp for 3 or 4 days to get medically examined and fixed up with kit and ration cards etc., then one month's leave on double rations and another on normal scale, and another medical examination on return to unit. News that typhus has broken out in Brunswick.

19 April. Got up early but the move was cancelled after the next Bn had moved up to the aerodrome. Packed my kit in morning. The postponement believed to be due to a break-through (General Patten) and the need for flying supplies up with all available troop-carrying aircraft. Spent a quiet day and ate very little food (fruit for breakfast, self-heating oxtail soup in morning, salmon mayonnaise for lunch, and a poached egg for dinner). Walked down to Pol Mazuelle with Bert after tea, and collected 2 letters from him to post from England. Arranged for him to collect milk, eggs, cheese, butter (?), cutlet of mutton (?), pork for us to collect tomorrow morning. Four POW contact offrs for the Dominions arrived in camp in afternoon. Read a *Daily Mirror* dated 13th of this month. Made cocoa in evening. Still got the 'squitters' but not feeling so bad as yesterday.

20 April. Sunny and warm day. Bert and I walked down to Pol Mazuelle and got a lift from a 'Deutsche' (with a pass!) for part of the way. Pol had not been out yesterday, and after a short wait we went out with him in a lorry to Bevenrode to collect eggs. However, this village was too near Oflag and there were many Indians there, so we went further into the country. Pol paid for what we got, but most refused the marks and I offered cigs to them. We got nearly 80 eggs (two dozen of which we left for Pol), 4 water-bottle-fuls of milk (one of which

135

we drank out there), and some white cream cheese. We also got some pork *fat* and a tin of pork which we left for Pol. Practically all the farms had only old men and women, and children in them plus a Pole. The latter seem to have stayed at their farms unlike other foreign workers. Most of the farms had already lost a lot of stock from armed Russians, and the inhabitants were petrified until they realized I was an English officer!! One took me for an Ite!! Enjoyed walking round the country very much – getting quite good at French now!! A Polish girl took Bert into a graveyard to show him the grave of her husband killed by the Nazis. Started walking back, but the truck caught us up (thank goodness!!) and dropped us a mile from the Oflag. Had over a pint of milk, some cold semolina and some bottled damsons for lunch at 3.00, when we got back. Feeling much better today, but taking food sensibly. Only had one 'rear' while we were out – in a 'lat' in a stable. Eating plenty of eggs and milk!! Visited Blackie at boiler-house in afternoon. News that we are moving tomorrow, and that this camp and aerodrome is to be used for repatriating POWs. Walked in woods with Bill Seymour in evening. Several planes landed on the aerodrome during the day. Saw big formations of Fortresses 'going home' in morning.

21 April. Early breakfast, but the move cancelled again!! I was Room 'stooge' and stayed in all day. Very good hot shower in morning. Rainy day and windy, but cleared up after tea. Finished reading *Garden Rubbish* and started *The Public School Question* by F.H. Spencer. Weighed myself – 56 kilograms, a *drop* of one kg in 6 days. However, Bert has gone down 2 kgs in a few days, and the difference must be due either to our recent exercise or to a fault in the hospital weighing-machine. My stomach is a bit more settled today. Cooked a little asparagus in evening. Many rumours about columns of a few German tanks and SS being destroyed north of here and not far away.

22 April. Early breakfast which I cooked, but the move postponed again – after 'B' battalion had walked up to the aerodrome for the 3rd day!! I had cooked some boiled eggs for the journey. Everyone fed up to the teeth with being messed about like this, having eaten their food and today's rain making walking unpleasant!! My stomach seems more upset today, and I am completely off my food. Slept part of

136

afternoon. Went to bed early and read a bit.

23 April. News that only 1,000 to move today (including us). Packed up ready etc., but did not get up early, as we have done lately!! Showery morning. Feeling much better but going easy on the tummy still!! Orders to move came after lunch and we moved to Waggun aerodrome. Set off (in our group of 25 including Jock, Bert, Sam and self) in a Douglas Dakota at 2.55. Crossed the Rhine at 4.10 and landed (very smooth landing) at Brussels at 5.00. The pilot warned us that it might be bumpy (and it was a little), but felt no ill effects and no one was ill in *our* plane. Sat at the front with Bert. Took boiled eggs and 2 biscuits on the trip. Showery weather, but very pleasant view. Saw quite a bit of bomb damage on the way. Also saw the gliders which were used in the 'Rhine Crossings'. Our planes had been carrying petrol (ie. not passengers) for their last few trips – pilot did not know why they were dropping us at Brussels and not taking us all straight to England. I think that more than the proposed 1,000 moved from Brunswick as the aerodrome was packed with Dakotas. On arrival at Brussels, we joined queue for tea, biscuits, hankies and cigs given free. Then we got in truck and were taken to a transit camp (ex-leave camp?) where we were disinfestated etc. (dodged it!!); then to Welcome Canteen for free tea and buns; and then to Document Office where we were detailed in drafts of 25 (Bert, Sam, Jock and I in 473), we were paid 800 Belgian francs and 10/- sterling, and were given (by Red X) a *free* 'gift bag' of toilet requisites, 2 bars chocolate, 2 hankies and 50 cigs (and socks etc., if required). All the rooms and the canteen were decorated with flags and welcoming slogans. A wonderful reception and organization, and very great kindness shown by *everyone* and especially by the women (Red X, YMCA, NAAFI etc., etc.) – the first *English* women we have spoken to for ages!! Then we went to our quarters and dumped our kit. I was carrying an 88 mm ammo box, a German Luftwaffe (?) pack and a haversack. We then went for a meal in the Mess – fresh beef, cabbage, etc., and a good sweet; 'civilized' food for a change, and very enjoyable (!!) and 1 pint of beer. Bert and I then filled in 'Interrogation Form'; and then walked down the beautiful avenue and excellent road towards Brussels, but did not go as far as the town. Very enjoyable to stroll about a street again (!!!), but it was getting dark by this time. Got back to hear

137

that Jock was staying behind at a hospital 'for his skin disease', but we learnt for certain tomorrow (from Bernie Kendrick) that he had T.B. We had thought this for months (due to his white face, unhealthy condition, his cough, his abnormal appetite, and the fact that he had let himself 'go to the dogs' ever since the autumn). When we got back, we heard of a stand-by order to move at 11.00 pm, but this was cancelled after we had brought our kit down to the Mess. Stayed in the Mess till quite late reading papers and magazines – wonderful to see English papers again! Saw 2 photos of the release of our camp and recognized 'Bull' Latham, Sandy Stewart, 'Click' Vanderson (pressman), and John Luntz. Kept bumping into the Kiwis who moved the same time as we, and did not 'lose' them till we set off again tomorrow.

24 April. Up very early (6.00-6.30?) – after a rather sleepless night – as we thought our group was called out on the loudspeaker to move (we were wrong!). Had breakfast (very good!!). Very cold in early morning. Went to Q.M stores, and got there before it was packed (especially Indians!!). We could take what we wanted free of charge. I got B.D. trousers (no blouse to fit), gaiters (too big!), boots, 1 pair of socks, kitbag and 2 towels. Then went to the 'Gift Shop', and after waiting in the queue I bought a good lipstick (180 Blg francs), silk stockings (120), scent (115), 2 hankies (140), and a lovely 'dog' (skin). The shop was run by Belgian women in some sort of uniform. Then went to 'Welcome Canteen' (as I also did last night) with Bert – very gaily decorated with flags, pictures etc, with tables, chairs, wireless, stoves etc. Tea, buns, sweets, cigs etc all given free. Read a few papers. Sat in hair-cut queue, but it was so slow that I had to leave as we were due to move at 11.00 am. About half of the remaining drafts moved at 11.00 (including most of Kiwis), and we were then 2nd in the draft 'queue'. Our move postponed. Given a pipe and tobacco by Red X. Haversack rations issued. I drew an extra 1,000 Blg francs, and went again to the 'Gift Shop' and bought 2 lipsticks (80), silk stockings (120), lighter (40), powder (60), scent (150). Tried the hair-cutting queue again, but the 'Stand to' order came over the loudspeaker!! Set off before 1.00 pm in 2 trucks (ie. only 2 drafts moving) to the aerodrome. By-passed Brussels, but saw a little bomb damage. Had to wait at aerodrome (wounded being unloaded). Drove round to a

NAAFI truck – tea, buns, cigs, free again!! Our two drafts (of 14 or 15?) set off in Dakotas at 3.10. A WAAF and a Canadian crew in ours. Saw the open fields with a 'strip' system of Belgium. Crossed the Channel coast at 3.55, and sighted England (nr Dungeness) at 4.05, crossing it at Rye a few minutes later. Very smooth journey but a *little* 'bumpy' over the Downs. Flew above the clouds most of the way (at one time 5500 feet up), but there were gaps in the clouds in most places (none over the Channel and very few over England) ('V' weapons?). Wonderful to see English scenery again over the Downs especially *green* trees, hedges, irregular fields etc. Landed at Dunsfold Aerodrome (nr Horsham which we flew over) at 4.40 pm. WAAFs shook hands and gave us 10 cigs each. Lovely smell of fresh grass etc. De-loused with 'powder gun'. A civilian padre carried my kit to a spacious and charmingly laid-out canteen decorated with flags and welcome signs, where we sat down to tea, sandwiches and cakes. The girls (forgotten what uniform they were in!) *would* insist on carrying our kit etc. Went by lorry to a Reception Camp (No 106, Barkfold – nr Kirdford, Billingshurst) after at first going to the 'wrong' place. Medical inspection for lice. Shown to very pleasant (nissen hut) billets, and sent official telegram home free. Very good hot shower and then meal in Mess. Collected a lot and filled in some forms re pay, claims etc. Got receipt for 590 Blg francs. We were paid £10. Drew 'Africa Star' and bought 2 pairs pants from Q stores. Was given D.W.R. cap badge. Lovely warm and fresh evening in grand surroundings. Telephoned home, but they could hardly hear anything at the other end, although the line 'this way' was good. Drew 6 weeks' NAAFI rations of cigs, matches, chocolates, sweets, razor blades, soap and note-paper, and paid for this in my Mess Bill (£1/4/6). Filled diary in in the Mess at night. Late to bed (sheets).

25 April. Re-packed after breakfast. Issued with ration cards (double for first 4 of the 6 weeks' leave), identification chit, 220 clothing coupons, and railway warrant. Had my hair trimmed. Transport arrived late (circa 11.30). Kit on lorry, and travelled in bus to Horsham. Got London train sometime after 12.00 and arrived London Bridge before 2.00. Travelled with Bert, Sam and Jack Ling. Parted in London. Took a taxi across to Kings Cross. I sent a telegram home. Dumped kit at

RTO's Store (after waiting in a queue), and then had a light meal at 'Lyon's Express'. Talked to a man at my table re the V2 damage. Bought sandwiches and caught the 4,00 train. Talked to a Polish airman (re Russia) on the train. Changed at Bradford and arrived Halifax about 10.20. Met by Daddy, Mummy and Peter. M and D unchanged, but Peter very tall and 'grown-up'. All the lights on in the house when we arrived and the flags out!! Rufus recognized me! Chicken and salad and baked custard waiting for me. Talked for some time, and then had a *'bath'*!!

26 April. Put Mufti on. Breakfast in kitchen. Talked most of the day!